D0105723

The Bumper Book of
Family Games

Published in the United Kingdom by
Collins & Brown
10 Southcombe Street
London
W14 0RA

An imprint of Anova Books Company Ltd

Distributed in the United States and Canada by Sterling Publishing Co. Inc.
387 Park Avenue South, New York, NY 10016

Copyright © Collins & Brown, 2012

Cover and interior illustrations © Advertising Archives, Bridgman Art Library & Corbis

All rights reserved. No part of this publication may be reproduced, stored in a retrieval sys-
tem, or transmitted in any form, or by any means electronic, mechanical, photocopying,
recording or otherwise, without the prior written permission of the copyright owner.

ISBN 978-1-90844-933-7

A CIP catalogue for this book is available from the British Library.

10 9 8 7 6 5 4 3 2 1

Reproduction by Mission, Hong Kong

Printed and bound by Toppan Leefung Printing Ltd, China

This book can be ordered direct from the publisher at www.anovabooks.com

The Bumper Book of
Family Games

by
Kate Hewett & Jo Pink

COLLINS & BROWN

Contents

●●●●●●●●●●●●●●●

Classic Outdoor Games 10

Tag 12

Tails 13

Coast Guards and Smugglers 14

Bulldog 15

Back to Base 16

Top 10 Delicious School Dinners 18

Capture the Flag 20

Hide and Seek 22

Sardines 23

Rounders 24

Football Rounders 26

Snap! 27

Four Square 28

Quiz Time History 30

Bench Ball 32

Dodge Ball 33

Horse Basketball 34

Blind Man's Buff 36

Musical Chairs 37

Musical Statues 38

Balloon Race 39

Pin the Tail on the Donkey 40

The Farmer's in His Den 41

Simon Says 42

Beggar My Neighbour 43

Oranges and Lemons 44

Top 10 Girls' Names of the 1950s and Now 46

Pass the Parcel 48

The Chocolate Game 49

Dressing-up Race 50

Steal the Bacon 51

The Memory Game 52

I Went to the Shops 53

Treasure Hunt 54

Tin Can Alley 55

Sandcastles 56

Beach Olympics 58

Bucket Relay Race 59

Water Balloon Toss 60

Limbo 61

Rock Pooling 62

Boules 65

Quiz Time Science & Nature............ 66

Ultimate 68

Clapping Games 70

Cheat................................ 71

French Skipping 72

Skipping 74

Grandmother's Footsteps 76

Mother, May I?....................... 77

Marbles 78

Hopscotch........................... 79

Top Ten Playground Rhymes.......... 80

Classic Car Games...................... 82

The Animal Game 84

So, What Am I Counting? 85

Alphabet Sequences 86

Red Car! 88

I Spy................................. 89

The Traffic Light Game 90

Car Treasure Hunt.................... 91

Pub Cricket 93

Quiz Time Sport...................... 94

Silent Counting 96

Bing Who? 97

Who Am I? 98

What Am I? 99

The Next Car Will Be... 100

Abstract Questions 102

Old Maid 103

Top 10 The Car's the Star! 104

Top 10 Amazing Car Facts 105

Waving Chicken 107

Quietest in the Car 108

Go Fish 109

Mimes 110

Car Poetry 112

Weird Vacations 114

When I Went on Holiday 115

Quiz Time Entertainment 116

Opposites 118

Backwards Spelling 119

The Janitor's Dog 121

Letter Word Tag 122

Knock-out Whist 123

DropOut 124

Top 10 Pioneers of Motoring! 126

Classic Indoor Games............... 128

Mummies 130

Light and Shade 131

Blindfold Drawing 132

Deadpan 133

Feelers 134

Noises Off 135

Squeak Piggy Squeak!.................... 136

Top Ten Excuses For Not Doing Homework 138

Murder in the Dark 140

I Have Never................................. 142

Wink Murder 143

In the Manner of the Word 144

Charades..................................... 146

Dumb Crambo 148

Top Ten Boys Names of the 1950s and Now.... 150

Consequences 152

Beetle 154

Noughts and Crosses...................... 155

Boxes.. 156

Battleships................................... 158

Quiz Time Geography 160

Twenty Questions 162

Botticelli 164

Buzz, Fizz, Fizz-Buzz.................................... 166

Chase the Ace 167

The Yes/No Game 168

Taboo.. 169

Top Ten Knock, Knock Jokes 170

Tiddlywinks 172

Pass the Orange 174

Paper, Scissors, Stone 175

Duck, Duck, Goose..................................... 176

Fish Flap 177

Quiz Time Art and Literature 178

Hangman 180

Are You There, Moriarty? 182

Bulls and Cows.. 184

Top Ten Driving Songs 186

Rummy 188

Quiz Time Answers...................................... 190

Acknowledgements 192

Classic Outdoor Games

●●●●●●●●●●●

Most of these games require lots of space for running around, throwing balls and acting silly. They're perfect for getting out all that restless energy and enjoying the sunshine. Make sure to bring a friend, outdoor games are best with large groups!

Tag

I knew this game as 'It' – isn't it funny how the best games are often the most simple?

How to Play

Tag can be played with two or more people – but generally the more the merrier. One person is 'It' and chases and tries to catch the other players. When they catch someone that player becomes 'It', and so on. It's helpful to include a rule that if you are caught you are not allowed to immediately tag the person who caught you, to stop the game from getting repetitive.

Name-Calling

You may also know this game as 'It', 'Tig', 'Tick' or 'Catch'.

> ## ✳ Variation
>
> • In 'Off-ground Tag' the people being chased are safe if they can find a place that is off the ground, e.g. a tree trunk, a climbing frame or a bench.
> • 'Kiss Chase' is another version of this game where the boys are all 'It' and have to chase the girls until they can catch and kiss them (or vice versa).

Tails

Adding tails is a good way to add a bit of variety to a game of 'It'. Tails can be made from anything – ribbons, string, fabric or rope – whatever you can find.

How to Play

Choose one person to be 'It' and give the other players a 'tail' to tuck into the waistband of their pants/skirts. When the game starts the person who's 'It' chases the others and tries to snatch their tails. If a player's tail is caught then he or she is out of the game.

And the Winner Is ...

The last person with a tail.

✳ Variation

This can be made into a team tag game. One example is 'Cat and Mouse'. In this game a small number of catchers or 'cats' chase the rest of the players, the 'mice', and try to snatch their tails. When all the tails have been caught the cat with the highest number wins.

Coast Guards and Smugglers

This is a brilliant game to play in the woods or in sand dunes with lots of scrub.

How to Play

Divide the players into two teams: a small number of 'coast guards' (2–3) with everyone else as 'smugglers' (8 or more). The coast guards then set up a base to be the 'jail'.

The coast guards shut their eyes and count to 30 so that the smugglers can run away and hide. The coast guards then have to catch all the smugglers. Smugglers are caught when a coast guard 'tags' them, and they are then automatically sent to jail. They can only be freed from jail if they are tagged by another smuggler that is still free. If time runs out and the smugglers have not all been caught, points can be awarded for the number of smugglers in jail.

> ☞ **Playing Tip**
> ●
> If there are lots of potential hiding places it may help to have a few more coast guards, so that the smugglers don't have too much of an advantage.

Bulldog

A few bumps were part and parcel of this game. I just used to shut my eyes, run for it and hope for the best!

How to Play

For five to 25 players. One member is the 'bulldog' in the middle of the playing area. The other players line up in a designated 'safe' area at one end. When the bulldog shouts 'Bulldog!', all the players run from one end of the playing area to the safe area at the other end without being caught.

To catch someone, the bulldog has to hold on to a player for as long as they take to shout '1, 2, 3, bulldog!' This player then joins the bulldog in the middle and helps to catch the players on the next run. The winner is the last to be caught.

Name-Calling

You may also know this game as: 'Red Rover', 'British Bulldogs', 'Cock-a-Rooster' or 'Pom-Pom-Pull-Away'.

" Jokes We Used To Tell "

Patient: Doctor, Doctor, I keep thinking I'm a pair of curtains.

Doctor: Pull yourself together!!

Back to Base

I went to four different elementary schools and this game was popular at each of them – albeit with slightly different names. I even played it at university!

How to Play

For three or more players. First everyone agrees on a base – like a tree, a rock or a wall – that players can touch back to and be safe. The person who's 'It' (the finder) covers their eyes and counts to 100. He or she then goes to find the hiders.

When a hider is spotted, he or she races back to touch base before the finder while shouting 'Back to Base 1-2-3!' If the finder reaches base first, then the hider is out.

While the finder is creeping around trying to seek out all the hiding places, the hiders have to look out for an opportunity to race back to base. The first person to get back to base is 'It' for the next game.

Watch Out For

Sneaky players hiding just round the corner or a short distance away ready to jump out and touch base the moment the finder walks away.

✱ Variation

Caught players can be put into 'jail' – an agreed area near to the base but not blocking it. If a player gets back to base before 'It' then the caught players are freed and 'It' has to count again.

Top Ten
Delicious School
Dinners

Everyone remembers their school dinners, no matter if it was the savoury spam fritters or the sweet suet of spotted dick. Many old-school dinners sounded exotic too, which has helped us remember them – even if they didn't always taste that nice! These were my Top Ten canteen classics...

1 Iced finger buns

2 Spotted dick

3 Jam roly-poly

4 Traffic-Light Tarts

5 Semolina Pudding

6 Beef cobbler

7 Pink custard

8 Spam fritters

9 Tapioca

10 Toad in the Hole

Capture the Flag

This used to feel like proper medieval warfare – we were brave soldiers defending our flag and our honour!

You Will Need
Two flags or other portable markers.

How to Play
You will need a playing area the size of, at least, a soccer pitch and then split the players into two even teams of five or more. Each team then decides on a base or 'jail' and a place inside the game's boundary to plant their 'flag', which can be an actual flag or just a marker. The teams must show one another where their flags have been placed. The aim of the game is to capture the other team's flag.

Once the flag has been placed, the defending team has to stay at least 5m (16ft) away from it to allow the opposing team the opportunity to capture it. During the game there is a safe area of about 10m (33ft) around each base. Make sure the safe areas are clearly understood by each team to avoid disagreements!

☞ Playing Tip
Teams can appoint certain members to be jailers, roaming guards or attackers.

Taking a 'Life'

Starting from their own bases, players must try to capture the other team's flag. If they touch or tag a member of the opposite team who is trespassing within their safe area, the trespasser loses a life and is sent to 'jail', only to be freed if they are tagged by a free member of their own team. The freed player must then go back to his or her own base to get another life before rejoining the game.

If a player captures the flag of the opposing team but is tagged on the way back to base, the flag must be left at that spot, and the defending players must stay 5m (16ft) away as before.

The Winner

The winning team is the one who captures the other team's flag and gets it back to their base or, if time has run out, the team who has managed to catch the most members of the opposing team.

" Jokes We Used To Tell "

What do you call a deer with no eyes?

No idea.

Hide and Seek

An all-time classic. Isn't it funny how loud your breathing sounds when you're hiding?

How to Play

Can be played with two players, but more is definitely better. One person is the seeker, while everyone else hides within a designated area. The seeker then covers his or her eyes and counts up to an agreed number to give everyone time to hide. When the seeker finishes counting they shout, 'Coming, ready or not!' When a person is found they are out immediately, they don't need to be tagged or caught. The game continues until the last person is found and this person is the winner.

✱ Variation

'Hide the Object', perhaps better known as 'Hunt the Thimble', is a game where the person who is 'It' hides an object (usually a small one, like a thimble) and the other players have to find it. The object can either be hidden or placed in plain sight. If players need a hint you can tell them whether they are 'warm' or 'cold'.

Sardines

This is Hide and Seek in reverse. It would often end with funny hiding positions and stifled giggles!

How to Play

One person hides while the rest count to a prearranged number. When the time's up the players go in search of the hider. When a player finds the hider, instead of ending the game by telling everyone else, he or she quietly squeezes into the hiding place, too.

Last One Standing

The loser is the last one to find the hiding place – by which time the other players will be squashed together like sardines. The loser usually then has to hide first in the next round.

" Jokes We Used To Tell "

What does Batman's mother call when it's time to come and eat?

Dinner dinner dinner dinner, BATMAN!

Rounders

Much as I hate to blow my own trumpet I used to be a bit of a Rounders queen and a pretty useful bowler to boot. I have to admit, though, it did represent the pinnacle of my sporting career.

You Will Need
A bat, a ball, six markers, such as cones or stumps.

How to Play
Divide players into two teams of about nine: this gives the fielding team a bowler, a backstop (to stop the ball when it goes behind the hitter), a fielder for each of the four bases, and three outfielders

Arrange four of the markers in a square within the playing area, which needs to be about 17m (56ft) deep, to mark out the bases, allowing about 12m (40ft) between each base. Then place one marker between bases 1 and 4, a few paces towards the centre of the square, where the batter should stand, and another marker a few paces closer still to the centre of the square, for the bowler. Toss a coin to see which team will bat first. The winning team is the one which scores the most rounders.

Batting
Each player on the batting team takes it in turn to hit the ball far enough so that he or she has enough time to run around the outside of all four bases before the ball is returned to the bowler. If this is achieved the player scores a 'rounder'.

If the batter doesn't have time to complete a rounder before the ball is returned from the outfield, he or she may stop at bases 1, 2 or 3; they will then run on to complete the circuit when the next or subsequent batter has started running. You can run even if you don't hit the ball – just make sure you reach first base before the backstop can throw it there!

When the ball is hit behind the batter, he or she can only run as far as first base. If you have only one bat it must be dropped (not thrown) inside the batting area for the next batter to pick up.

Bowling

A 'good ball' is bowled underarm and must reach the batter below head level, above knee level and within reach of the outstretched rounders bat. A ball bowled outside this area is a 'no ball'. A batter can hit a no ball if he or she chooses. This can be an advantage as you cannot be caught out from a no ball. Alternatively, the batter can ignore the no ball and wait for the bowler to bowl a good ball.

How to Be Out

A batter is out if a fielder catches the ball he or she has hit before it touches the ground, if the fielder touches the post the batter is running to with the ball before the batter reaches it, or if he or she leaves a post before the subsequent batter has started to run. He or she must remain in contact with the post at all times when not actually running and cannot return to a post already left behind. When all the players are out the teams swap places.

✱ Variation

Some games might include the opportunity to score a 'half rounder' by getting all the way round but stopping at one or more bases.

Football Rounders

Who needs a bat? Here are some ways to enjoy the excitement of Rounders even if you don't have the keys to the sports cupboard.

You Will Need
Football or similar-sized ball, six markers.

How to Play
The rules of this game are the same as for Rounders, but the bowler rolls the ball underarm along the ground and the 'batter' kicks the ball instead of trying to hit it with a bat.

✳ Variation

- Throwing Rounders is played without a bowler or a backstop. The 'batter' or 'thrower' stands on the batting spot and throws the ball as far as they can, then tries to run around as many bases as possible before being run out.
- In Danish Rounders the 'batter' hits the ball with his or her hand. They can't stop at bases and must try and score a rounder on each throw.

Snap!

The great thing about Snap! is that it can be simplified for younger players making it a straightforward matching game; this version, however, is fast, furious, physical – and noisy!

What do you need?

Play time!

10 mins per game

- 2–8 players.
- Usually one pack of cards is enough, but for a larger group you may need two.

Playing the game

The dealer shuffles and hands out all the cards evenly among the players face down so each player has their own pile in front of them.

The player to the left of the dealer goes first, and play then moves clockwise.

On his or her turn, each player turns over the top card from their face-down pile and creates a second, discard pile. Play continues until one player's card matches the value of a card on another person's discard pile, the first player to shout 'Snap!' wins both piles and adds them to his or her face-down pile.

Play continues until one player wins all of the cards; or, after a given amount of time, the player with the most cards wins.

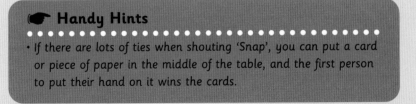

☞ Handy Hints
••
- If there are lots of ties when shouting 'Snap', you can put a card or piece of paper in the middle of the table, and the first person to put their hand on it wins the cards.

Four Square

Like many apparently simple games, some players have elevated Four Square to an art form. These are just the basics.

You Will Need

Chalk to mark out the playing area, a large ball such as a football or volleyball, an asphalt area like a playground.

How to Play

This is a game for four players at a time, although other players can wait on the sidelines to be swapped in. Draw a square 2.5m x 2.5m (8ft x 8ft), and divide it into four equal squares. The top left square is number 1, top right is number 2, bottom right is number 3, and bottom left is number 4. The object of the game is to gain the number 1 square and defend the position against the three attackers. The number 1 square is sometimes called the 'King' while the others (in descending order of importance) are the 'Queen' (2), 'Prince' (3) and 'Princess' (4). Each of the four players guards his/her own square. Decide between you who gets to start in each square, or you can draw lots. The number 1 player or King serves the ball by bouncing it in his or her square once and then hitting it with an open hand towards one of the other squares. The receiving player allows the ball to bounce in his or her square and then hits the ball to any other player. Play continues until one of the following things occur:

- A player hits the ball (or is hit by the ball) before it bounces once in their square.
- A player does not hit the ball before it bounces twice.
- A player hits the ball and it bounces outside of the playing area.

When one of these situations occurs the player concerned moves to the lowest ranking square and the other players then move up to higher ranking squares to fill the vacancies. If there are more players than squares, the player must leave the game and go to the back of the line, and the person at the front of the line moves onto the lowest square and starts to play.

" Jokes We Used To Tell "

How did the dinner lady get an electric shock?
She stepped on a bun and a currant went up her leg!

Quiz Time
History

History was my favourite subject at school. Inspired by my teacher, who flew a Spitfire in World War II and told us his flight plans were written on rice paper so he could eat them if he was captured, I was hooked from the age of 10! Now it's your turn.

1 What is the name of the illustrated record of the Battle of Hastings in 1066?

2 Which city was believed to be founded in 753 BC?

3 Which treaty brought a formal end to World War I?

4 Which Ancient Greek physician is known as 'The father of modern medicine'?

5 Which monarch was executed in the English Civil War (1642–1651)?

6 Who made his first major voyage of discovery in 1492?

7 What does the 'D' stand for in Franklin D. Roosevelt?

8 How many of Henry VIII's wives were called Catherine?

9 The Crimean War (1853–1856) was fought by Britain and France against which other country?

10 Which country was divided by the 38th parallel after World War II?

Check the answers on pages 190-191.

Bench Ball

Make sure your gym shoes have plenty of grip for this one — especially if you're the one on the bench!

You Will Need
Two benches and a large ball like a netball.

How to Play
Put a bench along each end of the playing area — usually the size of a badminton court (13.4m x 6.1m/44ft x 20ft). Divide the players into two teams of 6–12, with one team on each side of the court (if you do not have a centre line then you can use cones or markers instead). Each team chooses a goalkeeper who stands on one of the two benches.

The teams score goals by passing the ball to their own goalkeeper, while he or she is standing on the bench, without it being caught by the other team. To start the umpire throws up the ball between two opposing players. The players then pass the ball between themselves until someone shoots. A goal is only valid if the goalkeeper catches the ball while standing firmly on the bench — not while falling off!

When a goal is scored the opposition restarts by throwing the ball in from the goal line (behind the bench where the goal was scored). Once a goal has been scored a different player must become the goalkeeper.

Dodge Ball

We played this a lot in gym lessons on wet days – I used to pull my socks up high to try and avoid bruises!

You Will Need
A large ball like a football – but not too hard!

How to Play
Best for ten or more players. Choose two or more players, depending on how many there are in total, to be 'taggers'; the rest spread out within the playing area. The object is to tag the other players by hitting them with the ball below the knee. Only the taggers can pick up the ball. When players are tagged they are out and have to sit to one side. The last person remaining is the winner.

Name-Calling
You may also know this game as: 'Knee Ball', 'Ball Tag'.

✳ Variation
- In some versions the taggers can run with the ball, while in others they must stand still while they are holding the ball.
- Instead of sitting out when caught, players become taggers instead.
- This can be played as a team game with one team forming a circle of taggers while the other team moves about inside it. When a player is caught he or she can either sit out or join the opposing team and try and tag the people still inside the circle.

Horse Basketball

This game requires quite a lot of skill – I was never very good at it and would have to be awarded a lot of bonus shots to have any chance of staying in!

You Will Need
A basketball and a hoop.

How to Play
This is a game for two or more players. For two players toss a coin to decide who's going to go first; with more players you will need to decide on an order of play.

The first player takes a shot at the hoop from anywhere they choose on the court. If they make the shot then the second player has to make the same shot from the same position on the court.

If both players manage it the play passes to the next player (or back to the first player if there's only two) who selects a new shot for the next round.

If a player misses a shot, they are assigned the first letter of the word 'horse', i.e. 'H', and the other player selects the shot in the next round. As play continues each missed shot collects the next letter in the word horse. Once a player has collected all the letters then he or she is out of the game.

Play continues until only one player is left and they are the winner.

> ## ✱ Variation
> ●
> The word 'pig' can be used instead of 'horse' for a shorter game, or 'donkey' for a longer game.

Blind Man's Buff

This game was great fun but when I was blindfolded I would always worry that my friends were going to trick me by leaving the room without me realising!

You Will Need
A blindfold.

How to Play
One person is chosen to be 'It' and is blindfolded. He or she then walks around the room trying to tag the other players while they dodge around trying to avoid being caught. The person who is tagged is either out or becomes 'It' for the next round. Alternatively the game can continue until there's only one player left and he or she is the winner.

> **✳ Variation**
>
> After tagging someone, 'It' can feel their face and attempt to identify him or her; only if the tagged person is correctly identified does he or she become 'It'.

Musical Chairs

Fast, furious and competitive. My trick was to try and watch whoever was operating the music to see when they were going to hit the pause button.

You Will Need
Chairs – one fewer than there are people – and a music player.

How to Play
Arrange the chairs back to back in a line. All the players stand in a circle around the chairs. Agree in advance which direction to go, and then when the music starts walk, march or dance around the chairs. As soon as the music stops each player needs to find an empty chair and sit down as quickly as possible. The player left without a chair is out.

For the next round take one chair away and do the same again. Continue until there is just one chair and two players. When the music stops the first player to sit down is the winner.

✱ Variation
'Islands' is a similar game that uses newspaper instead of chairs. Spread out sheets of newspaper (one for every five players) and scatter them around the floor of the room. When the music stops, everyone has to squish together and stand on a piece of newspaper. Anyone not standing on newspaper after a few seconds (or failing that, the last person to get on the newspaper) is out. Every few rounds remove a sheet of newspaper, and when there's only one sheet left fold it in half until only one person is left – the winner.

Musical Statues

Standing still should have been an easy thing to achieve, so why did we always used to find it so hard? Maybe all that sugar had something to do with it!

You Will Need
A music player.

How to Play
When the music starts the players dance around the room. When it stops they must immediately 'freeze' while the judge (usually a grown-up) has a good look around to see who is wobbling. Anyone caught moving before the music starts again is out. The game keeps going until only one person is left, and they are the winner.

✱ Variation

In 'Musical Bumps' the players have to sit down on the floor when the music stops. The last person to sit down in each round is out and the last one left in is the winner. Be careful not to land too hard!

Balloon Race

This game was guaranteed to produce three things: lots of noise, burst balloons and red faces.

You Will Need
Lots of balloons – one for each team and plenty of spares!

How to Play
A game for two (or more) teams of four-plus people. Each team forms a line, the first player holds the balloon between their knees and passes it to the next player in the line without using their hands. When the balloon gets to the end of the line that player runs (as best they can!) to the front of the line with the balloon still between their knees and the process starts again. Play continues until the person who started returns to the front of the line and the team then sit down. The first team to sit down is the winner.

> ## ✱ Variation
>
> Instead of using their knees the first player passes the balloon backwards over his or her head, the next player then passes it between his or her legs to the person behind, who passes it over his or her head, and so on.

Pin the Tail on the Donkey

I loved the moment when I got to take off my blindfold and see where I had put the tail – I'm not sure I ever managed to get it in the right place!

You Will Need

A large picture of a donkey (or other animal with a tail); tails (pieces of rope or wool will do), sticky tape, a pin or adhesive putty at one end; a blindfold or scarf; a pencil to write each player's name next to their tail when they have placed it.

How to Play

Blindfold the first player and turn them around three times, then give them the tail, making it clear which is the sticky end. Guide them towards the picture so they can try and stick on the tail. The player who gets closest is the winner.

☛ **Playing Tip**

Touching the donkey where the tail needs to be placed before your turn will help you remember how high you will have to raise your arm.

The Farmer's in His Den

Circle games like this are always fun for young children.

How to Play

Choose one player to be the Farmer while the rest form a circle around him or her. The players in the circle hold hands and walk around the Farmer singing:

The farmer's in his den, the farmer's in his den,
E-i-adio, the farmer's in his den.
The farmer wants a wife, the farmer wants a wife,
E-i-adio, the farmer wants a wife.

The farmer chooses one of the other players to join him inside the circle as his 'wife'. The song starts again, but with the words, 'The wife wants a child …' and another player is chosen to go inside the circle as the 'child'. The song continues with 'The child wants a dog …' and then 'The dog wants a bone …' (and any others you can remember!) with a new player being chosen to join the farmer each time. The game ends with 'We all pat the dog …' and the players all pat the head of the player that has been chosen to be the dog.

Simon Says

Dating back hundreds of years, this game has been played in a variety of forms all over the world, in countries as diverse as Brazil, Finland, China and India.

How to Play

Choose one player to be Simon while the rest of the players line up about 4m (12ft) away. Simon then gives commands to the players, such as, 'Simon says, put your hands on your head'. He or she then checks to make sure everyone has followed the instruction correctly. Then Simon might say, 'Simon says, stand on one leg'. If Simon gives an instruction without first saying 'Simon says' then all those who follow it are out of the game. The winner is the last player remaining.

How to Catch People Out

- Give the orders quickly, one after the other.
- Cut the orders short, saying 'Simon says do this', and get the players to copy your action. Do this a number of times and then say 'Do this' – and quite a few people will usually follow your lead.
- Make it appear as if you are not playing the game for a moment and say something like, 'Can you come a bit closer?'. Sneaky, I know …

Beggar My Neighbour

This game is all about anticipation and luck, so everyone has an equal chance of winning.

What do you need?

- 2–4 players.
- One pack of cards.

Play time!

20 mins

Playing the game

The dealer shuffles and hands out all the cards evenly among the players so each player has their own pile in front of them, face down. The player on the left goes first and turns over their top card and places it in the middle of the table. If the card has a value between two and ten (these are 'ordinary' cards) play passes to the left and the next player does the same.

When the card played is a face card (a 'pay' card) the next player must make the following 'payments', placed face up, one at a time, on the pile:

- **Ace** four ordinary cards
- **Queen** two ordinary cards
- **King** three ordinary cards
- **Jack** one ordinary card

The player taking the 'payment' then picks up the whole of the central pile and adds it to the bottom of his or her face-down pile. However, if the 'payment' cards include a face card, then the player making the payment stops and the next player along must make the relevant payment, and so on.

Play continues until one player wins all of the cards; or, after a given amount of time, the player with the most cards wins. If a player runs out of cards, he or she must drop out of the game, while the others carry on.

Oranges and Lemons

This traditional game is based on the old English rhyme referring to the bells of several churches around the City of London.

How to Play

Facing each other, two players hold each other's hands and lift them up to form an arch. The other players form pairs, line up and walk through the arch while singing this song:

Oranges and lemons
Say the bells of St Clements.
You owe me five farthings
Say the bells of St Martins.
When will you pay me?
Say the bells of Old Bailey.
When I grow rich
Say the bells of Shoreditch.
When will that be?
Say the bells of Stepney.
I do not know
Says the great bell at Bow.
Here comes a candle to light you to bed
Here comes a chopper to chop off your head
Chop, chop, chop, chop
The last man's head!

The pairs keep filing through the arch until the song reaches the last two lines. At this point the players making the arch start making a chopping action with their arms, and on the last word – 'head!' – they catch the pair who happen to be passing through. This pair then forms another arch alongside the original pair, making it harder for the remaining players to escape the next round, and so on. The last pair left are the winners.

Top Ten
Girls' Names of the
1950s and Now

You only have to watch ten minutes of TV to realise that the most common, traditional names of the 1950s are gradually dying out, making room for a wider variety of names than ever before. A huge difference, but still lots of beautiful girls' names nonetheless!

1950	Now
1 Margaret	Olivia
2 Linda	Ruby
3 Mary	Chloe
4 Susan	Emily
5 Deborah	Sophie
6 Barbara	Jessica
7 Joan	Grace
8 Christine	Lily
9 Patricia	Amelia
10 Carol	Evie

(Office of National Statistics, 2010)

Pass the Parcel

Now I have my own children I've discovered just how long it takes to wrap the parcel for this game – I have now thanked my mother all over again for the many parcels she prepared for my parties over the years.

You Will Need
A prize wrapped in one more layer of wrapping paper or newspaper than there are players, and a music player.

How to Play
All the players sit on the floor in a circle. When the music starts the parcel is continuously passed around. Holding on to the parcel while the music is still playing is strictly forbidden!

When the music stops, the person holding on to the parcel removes one layer of paper. The music starts again and the parcel is passed around until the next time the music stops. When the parcel is down to its final layer the person holding the parcel when the music stops this time wins the prize.

" Jokes We Used To Tell "

How does an elephant hide in a cherry tree?

He paints his toenails red.

The Chocolate Game

I was always desperate to do well in this game, but with so many goodies to look forward to at teatime, this now seems rather surprising.

You Will Need
A big bar of chocolate; a knife and fork; a hat; a scarf; a pair of gloves; a die.

How to Play
All the players sit in a circle with the chocolate, knife and fork, and clothes in the middle. One player starts by rolling the die, which is then passed to the next person in the circle to throw, until someone throws a six. This person then has to put on the hat, scarf and gloves as quickly as he or she can and then, using the knife and fork, tries to eat as much of the chocolate as possible before the next person throws a six.

The game continues until all of the chocolate has been eaten – or until the players start to feel ill!

" Jokes We Used To Tell "

What goes up when the rain comes down?

An umbrella.

Dressing-up Race

This is basically a relay race with a difference – the difference is that this is a lot funnier.

You Will Need

For each team you will need an assortment of clothes (hats, scarves, gloves, raincoat, boots) and three markers (cones are good).

How to Play

Divide the players into teams of three or more. For each of the teams place one of the markers on the starting line, another one 3m (10ft) away on a mid-line with the pile of clothes, and a third 3m (10ft) further away on an end line that the players have to touch before returning to the mid-line and taking off the clothes.

When someone says 'go', the first player in each team runs to the mid-line and puts on all of the clothes. He or she then run to the end line or around the marker, then runs back to the mid-line, takes off the clothes, and then races back to the start line to tag the next person in the team who then does the same. They keep going until all the players have completed the race.

The winner is the first team to finish.

Steal the Bacon

Historically bacon was regarded as a valuable commodity, hence the phrase 'bringing home the bacon' when referring to a family's breadwinner! Perhaps this game derived from a less honest way of earning a living!

You Will Need
A bean bag, hat, scarf or other item to be the 'bacon'.

How to Play
You will need a leader and two equal teams of five or more players, who must stand in two lines facing one another, about 4.5m (15ft) apart. Place the 'bacon' in the middle.

The players of both teams are each given a number, starting with one (so that each number has two corresponding players, one in each team). When the leader calls out a number the two players try to run into the middle and snatch the bacon and get back to their line without being tagged by the opposite number. A successful bacon run wins a point for their team. If he or she is tagged then no one gets a point.

For a more challenging version of the game, the leader can call out a simple maths problem instead of just a number: for example, 'two times two', or 'five minus two'.

The team with the most points at the end of the game wins.

The Memory Game

This game first appeared in Kim by Rudyard Kipling and is named after the book's hero. It has since been adopted by the Scouting movement and by the military to help develop observational skills.

You Will Need
A tray of about 12 household items (such as a cup, saucer, ball of string, pen etc.); a cloth to cover it; pieces of paper and pens (one for each player).

How to Play
Put the tray where all the players can see it. Uncover the items and let the players memorise them for a minute. Cover the tray again with the cloth and then ask the players to write down as many items as they can remember for another minute. The winner is the player who remembers the most items.

* Variation
For younger children you can show the players the tray, ask them to close their eyes and then take one of the items away. When they open their eyes, the first one to shout out the name of the missing item wins that round.

I Went to the Shops ...

This is a classic memory game that used to be popular in schools as well as at parties. Well, they do say learning should be fun ...

How to Play

Everyone sits in a circle. Someone begins by saying, 'I went to the shops and bought ...' and chooses something beginning with the letter 'A', for example 'an apple'. The next person then says, 'I went to the shops and bought an apple ...' and then adds an item beginning with the letter 'B' and so on.

If you forget the order or get any item wrong then you're out. The last person left is the winner.

☛ **Playing Tip**

This game can get confusing, especially when people drop out. It often helps to look at each person while you're reciting the list, to help you remember what they said.

Treasure Hunt

This game was fun anyway, but the promise of a prize at the end made it even more exciting.

You Will Need

A selection of candy and prizes, or slips of paper containing clues that finally lead to the main prize or 'treasure'.

How to Play

The simplest treasure hunts can just involve looking for candy hidden around the house or garden. Whoever finds a candy gets to keep (or eat!) it.

More sophisticated hunts begin with a clue that leads to a location where there will be another clue, and so on. The clues might be straightforward ('The next clue is behind the chair') or more cryptic ('The next clue is behind something blue').

Or a treasure hunter might be given a map showing the location of the treasure and heads off, either alone or in a team, to try and find it.

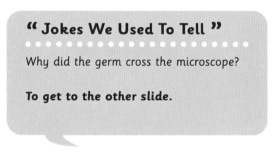

" Jokes We Used To Tell "

Why did the germ cross the microscope?

To get to the other slide.

Tin Can Alley

Just like a sideshow at the fairground, this game was a really fun way to develop your target skills.

You Will Need
Ten empty cans and some bean bags.

How to Play
For three or more players. Stack the cans in a pyramid on a table with four on the bottom, then three, then two, then one.

Each player is given three bean bags and must try and knock down all the cans – make sure the players are standing well enough back to make the game a challenge. If none of the players are able to knock down all the cans then the one that manages to knock down the most in each round is the winner.

✱ Variation
• As the game continues you can move the start line further and further back each time to make the game harder.
• You could also build the cans up again after each throw and add up the points scored each time.

Sandcastles

As a child the best thing in the world is knocking over a single sandcastle someone has built for you.

You Will Need

Spades, buckets, moulds, trowel. Plastic knives and lolly sticks are also useful for shaping smaller features.

How to Build a Sandcastle

If you want your sandcastle to last, its location is quite important – it needs to be near enough to the water's edge that the sand is damp enough to work with, but not so near that the waves come in and wash it away. Here are some basic elements to create a majestic sandcastle:

Towers build up the height of your towers using thick circular 'slices' of damp sand until you have the height you need.

Walls press handfuls of wet sand together in a line and then build them up layer by layer. The base needs to be wider to provide the proper support.

Arches these start off as walls and when they are ready use a small tool to start tunnelling through at the base, gradually making the hole bigger.

☞ **Playing Tip**

• If you want to be really sophisticated a spray bottle filled with water is useful to stop the sand from drying out.
• If using a bucket, when you are filling it up give it a shake every now and then to make sure there are no gaps, and then pack the sand down firmly.

Beach Olympics

This was always great fun but now I see that my parents had an ulterior motive – large amounts of physical activity for the children, while they sat around with drinks and stopwatches.

You Will Need
General beach stuff like buckets and spades, some belts or scarves for three-legged races, rope for tug of war, and a watch for timed events.

How to Play
First decide on your events. Here are some we tried:

Three-legged race decide on the start and finish line, and the first team to get there wins.

Long jump draw a line in the sand. All the players run to the line and jump. Whoever jumps the furthest is the winner.

Hurdles create some hurdles using spades, cool boxes, beach bags etc. Take it in turns to run the course, and the person with the fastest time wins.

Tug of war an old favourite. Playing on sand can be tricky – it's difficult to get a grip, but dig your feet down well and you should find it easier.

" Jokes We Used To Tell "

What did the ocean say to the shore?

Nothing, it just waved.

Bucket Relay Race

A game of persistence, concentration and teamwork.

You Will Need
One bucket for each team.

How to Play
Divide the players into two teams of three or more and line them up next to the shore. Put the buckets about 3m (10ft) from the water's edge.

The object of the game is for each team to fill their bucket using just their hands to hold the water. When the race starts the first member of each team scoops up a handful of water, runs to the bucket and drops the water in. They then run back to their team and the next player can go. The players keep going until the bucket is full, and the first team to fill their bucket is the winner.

> ## ✳ Variation
> Use a full bucket of water and have the teams run to a marker and back before handing the bucket to the next member of the team. At the end of the race the team that has spilled the least amount of water is the winner.

Water Balloon Toss

This is a great way to keep cool on a hot day.

You Will Need
Lots of water balloons, an even number of players (four or more).

How to Play
Divide the players into teams of two and give each pair a balloon. Get them to stand about 1m (3ft) apart. When the game starts the teams have to throw the balloons to each other, and with each successful catch the players have to take two steps back, making the distance between the players wider. The players must continue to move further and further apart with each throw.

How to Be Out
If the balloon bursts during play then the team is disqualified.

And the Winner Is ...
The last team with their balloon still intact.

> ## " Jokes We Used To Tell "
>
> What happened to the wooden car with wooden wheels and a wooden engine?
>
> **It wooden go.**

Limbo

There's something about beaches that makes us want to limbo dance – at least you have a soft landing!

You Will Need

A long stick, a length of ribbon or a skipping rope – basically anything that can be used as the limbo pole.

How to Play

A bit like the high jump in reverse. Two people need to hold the limbo pole or pull the rope taught.

Stand with your feet shoulder-width apart and your arms out. Using small, controlled movements, jump forwards towards the pole but don't start to bend until you reach it. Then bend your legs and lean backwards gradually as you move forwards under the pole. Wait until your head has passed under the pole and then gradually start to come up.

After each round the pole gets lower and lower. If you touch the pole or fall, you are out. The last one left in is the winner.

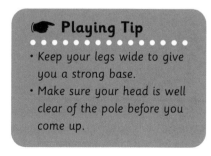

☞ Playing Tip

- Keep your legs wide to give you a strong base.
- Make sure your head is well clear of the pole before you come up.

Rock Pooling

A glorious pastime. I was lucky enough to spend childhood holidays on the unspoiled coast of south-west Ireland – a rock pooler's paradise.

You Will Need
Shoes or boots, preferably waterproof, with a good grip: rocks can be slippery and shells can be sharp so you must protect your feet.

How to Go Rock Pooling
Go down to the beach at low tide, find some rocks and start looking around. Watch out for the tide coming back in, as you don't want to get stuck with no way back to dry land; check the tide times when you arrive.

Remember:
- Watch carefully and quietly – many seashore creatures are hard to spot and they will hide themselves if they think you are a threat.
- You will find things on top of rocks, in cracks and crevices, under stones, on seaweeds and in rock pools. If you lift a stone to see what is underneath, make sure you put it back down.
- Every tiny detail of a rock pool is very important to the survival of one creature or another. Therefore, leave everything just as you found it and the rock pool creatures will be there for next time.

What to Look For
Here are some of the things you might find when rock pooling:

Limpets
You will find these round, ridged shells clinging to rocks. In fact they move around the rocks very slowly, eating the weeds that they pass over.

Barnacles
These tiny, white crustaceans cover the rocks in their thousands. At low tide they just look like shells, but under water a little 'fan' emerges to collect plankton.

Starfish
Less common but an exciting find.

Fish
Can become stranded in rock pools, and young fish sometimes stay there until they mature.

Crabs
These tend to live under stones and in crevices.

Anemones
At low tide these look like little blobs of jelly, but when the tide starts to come in their tentacles emerge in search of small prey like shrimps.

Seaweeds
You may see many different varieties, so count how many you can find.

Prawns and shrimps
Can be hard to spot as they are quick to sense and hide from curious onlookers.

Boules

Also known as pétanque, this is a great game to play on a beach.

You Will Need

A set of balls – three per player – and a smaller target ball or 'cochonnet'.

How to Play

Teams can comprise one, two or three players. Toss a coin to choose which team plays first. Any player in this team chooses where to draw a circle on the ground, in which each player will stand to throw their boules.

The same player then throws the cochonnet 4–8m (13–26ft) away from the circle in any direction, at least 1m (3ft) away from any obstacles.

Any player from this team then throws their first boule, trying to get it as close as possible to the cochonnet. When throwing a player's feet must stay together on the ground and inside the circle until the boule has landed.

A player from the opposing team then throws their boule from the circle, trying to get it closer to the cochonnet or knocking their opponent's boule away. The team with a boule closest to the cochonnet is 'Holding the point'.

The players in the team that is not 'holding' continue to throw until they place a boule closest to the cochonnet, and so on. Players on the same team do not have to alternate, but players must play their own boules.

When a team has no more boules throw, the players of the other team throw theirs and try to place them as close as possible to the cochonnet.

Scoring

When both teams have no more boules, you stop and count up the points. The winning team scores one point for each boule nearer the cochonnet than the opponents' closest. Only one team can score points in each round.

Quiz Time
Science and Nature

Biology, Chemistry, Maths – even double Maths – did not fill me with dread when I was at school. Physics, on the other hand, was another matter and I couldn't wait to give it up. Which of the sciences was your bête noire? Here are a few questions that might help you remember...

1 Diamonds are a form of which chemical element?

2 What is the longest bone in the human body?

3 Relating to flat-screen televisions and monitors, what does LCD stand for?

4 What is the mathematical series that starts 0,1,1,2,3,5,8,13,21 called?

5 Which sub-atomic particles are found in the nucleus of an atom?

6 Which sugar is found in milk?

7 Which is the largest species of big cat in South America?

8 What did Wilhelm Conrad Röntgen discover by accident on 8 November 1895?

9 In trigonometry, what is calculated by the adjacent over the hypotenuse?

10 What is the usual colour of copper sulphate?

Check the answers on pages 190-191.

Ultimate

Invented in the United States, Ultimate is a team game that uses a disc or Frisbee, with rules loosely based on American Football.

You Will Need
A Frisbee or disc.

How to Play
First determine your playing area. A standard Ultimate field is 37m (40 yards) wide and 110m (120 yards) long; the playing area is 64m (70 yards) long with end zones of 23m (25 yards) at each end, and a standard team has seven players. You can adapt your playing area (and the number of players) to the space available.

The teams decide who will throw first by flipping discs or by 'rock, paper, scissors'. When play begins the team throwing first (the defensive team) must be inside their end zone, and the opposing team (the offensive team) line up on their end zone line. Both teams need to signal their readiness to start by raising a hand, and then play begins with the defensive team throwing the disc to the other team.

Once a player catches or picks up the disc, he or she must stop and keep one foot planted as a pivot until the disc is passed to another player by throwing it (passing the disc hand-to-hand is not allowed). The player has ten seconds to pass the disc and this is counted down by a member of the defensive team, who must remain 3m (10ft) from the player with the disc. This also applies for the offensive team.

If any of the following occur possession transfers to the other team which then becomes the offensive team:

- the ten-second count expires without the player passing the disc.
- the disc is dropped when catching or during the possession.
- a pass is blocked, intercepted or not caught.
- the disc is thrown out of bounds.

Scoring

Goals are scored by a team successfully completing a pass to a player located in the defensive end zone. After a score, the teams switch their direction of attack, and the scoring team throws. Play continues until either team reaches 15 points with a two-point margin over their opponents, or until either team reaches a total of 17 points.

> **" Jokes We Used To Tell "**
>
> Which snakes are found on cars?
>
> **Windscreen vipers!**

Clapping Games

Why is it that you can't remember last week but you can remember a clapping song you learned when you were five?

How to Play

Clapping games are always played with a partner. Begin by clapping your hands together at the same time, then reach out with your right hand to clap your partner's right hand. Clap your hands again. Reach out with your left hand and clap your partner's left hand. Repeat. Always clap on the beat.

The next stage is to start with your left hand up and your right hand down with your partner mirroring you. On the first beat you clap down onto your partner's hands with your left hand and up with the right, on the second beat you clap your partner's hands in front of you, and on the third you clap your hands together. Repeat until the end of the song. This was one of my favourites:

Miss Mary Mack, Mack, Mack,
All dressed in black, black, black,
With silver buttons, buttons, buttons,
All down her back, back, back.
She asked her mother, mother, mother,
For 50 cents, cents, cents,
To see the elephant, elephant, elephant,
Jump over the fence, fence, fence.
He jumped so high, high, high,
He touched the sky, sky, sky,
And he never came back, back, back,
'Til the fourth of July, ly, ly!

Cheat

You have to have your wits about you when playing this game and a poker face certainly helps.

What do you need?

- 2–5 players for one pack of cards.
- 6–11 players with two packs of cards.

Play time!

20 mins

Playing the game

The dealer shuffles and hands out all the cards evenly among the players. To start, the player to the left of the dealer plays one or more cards from their hand, face down, to make a central discard pile in the middle of the table. They must announce the rank and number of the discarded cards. The first player starts with Aces, the second player Twos, and so on around the table.

However, as the cards are played face down, you do not actually have to discard the exact cards you are calling – you may not have any cards of a particular rank for example, and as the object of the game is to get rid of al your cards you will want to try and discard as many cards as you can.

Any player who suspects the cards being played are not the same as the rank that is called can make a challenge by shouting 'Cheat!'. When the cards are shown there are two possible outcomes:

1. The cards match the rank that was called. Then the challenging player must take all the cards on the discard pile and add them to their hand.
2. The cards do not match the rank that was called. Here the person who played the cards must take the discard pile and add it to their hand.

Play then starts again with the player to the left of the person that was challenged.

The first player to get rid of all their cards is the winner.

French Skipping

The cause of quite a few grazed knees as I recall. This was the game that everyone wanted to be the best at.

You Will Need
A length of elastic around 5mm (¼in) wide, and three players – or one player and two chairs if you're desperate!

How to Play
Two players stand facing each other with the elastic stretched quite tight around their ankles to form a long rectangle and the third player has to perform a series of jumps and hops, singing a rhyme at the same time. For example:

Peanut cookies, when you bake,
How many minutes will you take?
One, two, three, four, five.

On **'one'** the player has to jump up and land facing sideways with the right foot in the middle of the loop and the left foot outside.

On **'two'** they have to jump and land with the left foot in the middle and the right foot outside.

On **'three'** they have to jump and land with both feet outside the elastic.

On **'four'** they have to jump and land with both feet on top of the elastic.

On **'five'** it gets really hard as they have to jump and land with both feet outside the elastic then shuffle round to face the other way, so the elastic makes a zig-zag shape around their legs, then jump out and land with their feet on top of the elastic.

If they manage this tricky task, the elastic is raised to knee height for another round, then thigh height and finally waist height for French Skipping superstars. When they get it wrong, it's the next person's turn, and the first person has to start from scratch again next time.

Another popular chant was this one:

England, Ireland, Scotland, Wales,
Inside, outside, inside, on!

Skipping

One of my favourite school games that we just never seemed to get tired of. Although it was mostly the girls that played, you could guarantee that when the boys joined in they would try to show us who was best!

You Will Need

A regular rope for skipping by yourself or with a partner, a longer (7.5m/25ft) rope for playing in a larger group – and a loud voice for chanting.

Partner Games

These just use a regular skipping rope and usually one other person. The one I remember most is this one.

'I Like Coffee, I Like Tea'

Start off skipping on your own. As you skip, say the following rhyme, including your friend's name:

'I like coffee, I like tea, I like Julie in with me!'

Now your friend jumps in and skips with you and you say:

'I don't like coffee, I don't like tea. I don't like Julie in with me!'

Your friend must now jump out of your skipping rope as you skip. Keep going for as long as you can without stopping.

Group Games

For these games you need the longer rope and two people to turn it ('enders'). Our favourites included:

1. Bumper Car, Bumper Car

For this game you take turns to jump in and say:

Bumper car, bumper car number 48,
Went around the corner

(at which point you run out, around one of the enders and back in the other side),

And slammed on the brakes

(here you stop the rope between your legs).

2. Teddy Bear, Teddy Bear

One at a time, jump in and skip to this rhyme and do the actions described as you say it:

Teddy bear, teddy bear, turn around,
Teddy bear, teddy bear, touch the ground,
Teddy bear, teddy bear, go upstairs,
Teddy bear, teddy bear, say your prayers,
Teddy bear, teddy bear, switch off the light,
Teddy bear, teddy bear, say goodnight.

If you stop the rope or miss any of the actions you are out. When out, swap with one of the people turning the rope.

Grandmother's Footsteps

I always tried to make sure I was standing on two legs at all times – otherwise I would be sure to wobble.

How to Play

Choose one person to be Grandmother. She (or he) stands at one end of the playing area while the other players stand on a line (real or imaginary) about 10m (33ft) away. While Grandmother's back is turned the players try to sneak up on her but whenever she turns around the players have to freeze. Anyone who is caught moving must go back to the start. The first person to touch Grandmother takes over for the next round.

Name-Calling

You may also know this game as: 'Red Light, Green Light', 'Statues' or 'Sly Fox'.

" Jokes We Used To Tell "

What's black and white and red all over?

A newspaper!

Mother, May I?

Another one of my favourites – if your friend was 'Mother' you knew you had a good chance of winning!

How to Play

For three or more players. Choose one person to be 'Mother' (can be 'Captain' or 'Father' if boys don't want to be 'Mother'!). The rest of the group stands in a line facing them a fair distance away. Your aim is to reach Mother but you must take it in turns and can only move according to her instructions.

Mother gives instructions to each player in turn, for example, 'Olivia, take one giant and three baby steps'. Olivia must say, 'Mother, may I?' and then take her steps. If you forget to say 'Mother, may I?' or get the step wrong you must return to the start. The first player to reach Mother is the winner.

✳ Different Types of Steps

Baby steps (steps the exact length of your foot); regular steps; giant steps (the biggest steps you can make); bird steps (tiny steps with toes pointed out putting your heel halfway along the inside of the opposite foot for each step); bunny/frog steps (hops); banana step (where you lie down with your feet at their current spot, noting where the top of your head is, and standing up there for your new position).

Marbles

Who didn't love marbles – smooth, shiny and glittering like playground jewels!

You Will Need
Each player will need one large shooter marble (2cm/3⁄4in) and a selection of regular (1.5cm/5⁄8in) marbles. Chalk for drawing lines.

How to Play
For two or more players. Draw two circles on the ground: the inner circle should be about 30cm (1ft) in diameter and the outer circle about 2m (7ft). Players must agree on the number of marbles to be placed in the inner circle, and then they take turns to shoot their larger marble from any point on the outer ring at the marbles in the centre.

If the shooter knocks any of the marbles out of the inner ring he or she gets to keep them and to shoot again from where the shooter marble landed.

If the shot is unsuccessful the shooter marble stays where it is (if it is inside the outer ring) and play passes to the next player who may shoot at the marbles inside the inner ring or at any of the other shooter marbles. If a player strikes a shooter marble, the owner of that marble must give the shooter one of his or her marbles to get it back, and the shooter takes another shot. Play continues until the ring is cleared.

And the Winner is ...
The person with the most marbles at the end of the game. But are you playing 'Keepsies' (where the winners get to keep all the marbles they have won) or 'Fairsies' (where the winners get to keep all the marbles they have won)? Make sure you agree on this before you start the game.

Hopscotch

When I was at school this game got so competitive we tried to find the most accurate marker we could.

You Will Need
Chalk for drawing the grid, a stone or beanbag to be a marker.

How to Play
For two or more players. First mark out your grid. These do vary but the one shown here seems to be the most common.

Decide the order of play. The first player throws his or her marker into square number 1. They must then move along the grid hopping on one foot on single squares and planting two feet on double squares.

When they reach number 10 they turn around and come back using the same technique. When they reach their marker they pick it up and return to the start.

Remember:
- The beanbag must land within the square. If it lands outside the grid, on a different square or on the line of the square, it is considered a misthrow and you miss your go.
- When you are moving through the grid you must not land on the lines or outside the grid. If you do either of these you must return to the start and wait for your next go.
- If you put your other foot down when you are supposed to be on one leg you must return to the start.
- You mustn't put your foot in the square where your marker is.

Top Ten
Playground Rhymes

Whether you were clapping, skipping or just plain old running around, playground games have always been accompanied by wonderful chants and songs. Many of the rhymes below will come flooding back to you just by reading their title – it will then be days before you are able to get them out of your head!

1 Ring a Ring O'Roses

2 London Bridge

3 One Potato

4 Oranges and Lemons

5 Pat-a-cake, Pat-a-cake

6 Follow the Leader

7 Row, Row, Row Your Boat

8 Mary, Mary, Quite Contrary

9 Jack and Jill

10 She'll Be Coming 'Round the Mountain
When She Comes

Classic
Car
Games

• • • • • • • • • • •

You'd be surprised how much fun you can have while stuck in traffic! The whole family can get in on the fun (as long as they don't distract the driver!). Test your observation skills with What Am I Counting? and I Spy or get creative with Car Poetry. If you need a moment of peace you can always ask the children to play Silent Counting.

The Animal Game

For the animal game, you split the car into two halves. The right-hand side of the car takes the right side of the road, and the left-hand side of the car takes the left. This works well for a family of four, but it's up to parents how you split up three (or five) kids.

Whenever you spot animals in fields on your side of the road you have to count them out loud. So if you pass them too quickly, before you've got to fifteen – too bad!

The winner is the side who has counted the most animals.

You can continue it in town, too, with domestic pets being walked or cats that dare to cross the street.

✱ Variation

- If you're passing through an area with few farm animals you can adapt it to any four-legged animals you see, provided you can shout out what they are. Try including animals you see on billboards – again their names must be shouted out loud to score points.
- Instead of counting the animals out loud, you can make mooing, baaing or oinking noises. Great fun if there's more than one type of animal in the field!

So, What Am I Counting?

One player decides to count something outside. It could be street lights, telegraph poles, green signs, single-storey houses, ponds, dogs or roadkill. What they don't do is tell anyone what it is they're counting.

Instead, whenever they pass the object they've selected, they count out loud, adding to their score. The other players have to guess what it is that's being counted.

🚗 Playing Tip

To keep the game moving, ask players not to choose really rare things to spot – such as piebald horses, juggling sheep or houses with a ladder on the roof!

✳ Variation

If the object a player has chosen doesn't appear within the next three miles then they lose their go.

Alphabet Sequences

Number plates are a great source of game material. The the idea is to spot alphabet sequences. It works best if the whole car plays as one team.

So, to start the game players need to spot the letter "A" on a number plate, then it's "BTY" or "BCM" or, if they're really lucky, "BCD" all on the same number plate.

However "BMC" would only count as the letter "B" (because the "B" and the "C" need to be next to each other – unless you want to play the game at lightning speed).

✱ Variation

Split the car into two teams and have one team going backwards through the alphabet, from Z to A, while the other is working forwards, from A to Z. This works well as a race to finish spotting all the letters.

" Things Mums Say "

Do as I say, not as I do

Red Car!

A game that Henry Ford never imagined would happen (his famous motto was, "You can have any colour you like, providing it's black"). The Red Car game is simple. See who can spot a red car first. The person who spots it yells out, "Red car!" and gets a point. If they yell out "Red car!" and it's not, then it's minus a point.

Everyone has to see the red car for it to count.

Do maroon cars count? Yes
Do half-red cars count? Yes
Do red trucks count? No
Do cars with a red stripe count? It depends how big the stripe is.

🚗 **Playing Tip**
● ● ● ● ● ● ● ● ● ● ● ● ● ● ●
Darker colours are a
nightmare to adjudicate

✳ **Variation**
● ● ● ● ● ● ● ● ● ● ● ● ● ● ●
If you get bored of red,
there's always blue, green,
and yellow you can spot.

I Spy

A classic car game – one player secretly spots something on view to everyone in the car and then the other players have to guess what it is. For the very few that don't already know it, the person nominated starts by saying …

"I spy with my little eye, something beginning with S …"
The player who guesses correctly what that thing beginning with "S" is gets the next turn.

Playing Tip

Dedicated I Spy players will know that it's very easy to spot something outside of the car that all of a sudden gets left miles behind. So when the answer is finally uncovered there are cries of, "So where was that, then?"

To make sure everyone knows what the score is, best to get players to add if it's "inside" or "outside" of the car. That way, if it's outside, players can look around straight away.

The Traffic Light Game

In this simple game players have to guess how many traffic lights the car will go through on green before they get held up on red. All players guess at once and the person who gets closest to the right number wins.

Traffic Lights and Payphones is a much more involved game. Each player takes it in turn to own the car and tries to go through the most sets of traffic lights on green. If they hit a red light, their turn isn't always ended, as each payphone spotted between lights counteracts the next red. When a player runs out of payphones and hits a red light, their turn is over. The winner is the player who's passed the most traffic lights.

✱ Variation

This game can be played by the whole car or individual players.

You can carry over payphones from one set of lights to the next. If there are few payphones around, then a church or religious building can substitute.

Car Treasure Hunt

The Treasure Hunt game needs a small amount of preparation before you set off on your journey. For each child construct a list of 10 things they have to spot on the journey. You can even incentivize them with a chocolate-for-objects-spotted scheme ...

Each child has their own list and a pencil so they can cross off each item as they spot it through the trip.

The kind of things to watch out for will vary depending on what kind of countryside or urban landscape you're heading through. A mountain might be a good thing to spot if you are going skiing and a skyscraper might be handy if you're going on an inner city trip.

Here's some ideas of things you might include:

Fir tree	Orange car	Burger King
Dead tree	Stripy car	McDonalds
Fire engine	Alsatian dog	Ford showroom
Ambulance	Traffic cone	Cinema
Police patrol	Digger	Theatre
Bird of prey	Railway bridge	Church
Sheep	Goods train	Castle
Pig	Passenger train	Hotel
Horse	Red bus	Billboard
Pink car	School bus	Petrol station

Pub Cricket

First of all, you need a basic idea of what happens in cricket to play this game. Players take it in turns to be "in" or batting. Everyone then has to keep their eyes peeled for each pub that the car passes.

Most importantly they need to take a look at the pub sign to see how many legs are on it. For instance, if it's a pub called The White Horse, then it has four legs – and so the batsman scores four runs. If it's called The Coach and Horses, and there are two horses and a coachman in the picture, that's a total of 10 legs, so the batsman scores a massive 10 runs.

But if the picture has no legs – for example, The Crown, The Bell, or The Slug and Lettuce, they're out and it's the next player's turn.

" Jokes We Used To Tell "

Did you hear the joke about the magic tractor?

It turned into a field.

Quiz Time
Sport

Sport often takes viewing precedence above everything else in our house – does that sound familiar?

1 Which well-known soccer player's surname is Luis Nazario de Lima?

2 Who was the first gymnast to be awarded a perfect 10 at the Olympic Games?

3 In which city does American football team the 49ers play?

4 Which cricketer holds the record for the greatest number of runs scored in a single innings in a test match?

5 In cycling, who has set a record by winning six Tours de France in succession?

6 What's the name of the game played on broomsticks by Harry Potter and his friends at Hogwarts?

7 What are the three disciplines in Three-day Eventing?

8 Which athletics discipline was revolutionised by Dick Fosbury?

9 What number shirt is worn by a fullback in Rugby Union?

10 In golf, what term is given to completing a hole in two shots under par?

Check the answers on pages 190-191.

Silent Counting

How long does a second last? The time it takes to say "one thousand" or even "one elephant?"

Here's the challenge. Ask someone in the car to count out a minute silently in their heads. At the same time, someone with a second hand on their watch keeps note of the time. When the player thinks they've reached a minute they shout out, "NOW!"

How many seconds are they off their target minute? Try it again with everyone in the car and see who can get closest.

✳ Variation

- Two, three or even four players can play this at once with everyone shouting out when they think the minute is up.
- If you have three or more players give everyone a separate word, otherwise you won't know who's shouted out closest to the minute mark, whilst keeping your eyes glued to your watch!

Bing Who? (or The Bing Game)

This is a game that splits the car in two – grown-ups versus children. And the grown-ups' decision is final.

The basic version of the game is as follows: the children in the car have to shout out a first name and the grown-ups have to think of a famous person with that name.

They can be celebs, sports stars, fictional characters from books, television and movies or even relations.

For every person the grown-ups name, they get a point – for every person they fail to name the children get a point.

✳ Variation

Grown-ups, give yourselves five Time Outs for when the little rascals think up something fiendish, if you want to stack the odds in your favour.

Because the game requires a good knowledge of famous people, children are at a disadvantage in doing the naming, but they can always play among themselves if they are evenly matched.

Who Am I?

This game involves guesswork and asking the right questions.

One player chooses a person that they know, and that the other passengers in the car know. They don't reveal who it is.

Now it is up to the rest of the players to ask a series of questions that reveal their identity. All the choosing player must answer is "yes" or "no". So the interrogation could proceed along the lines of:

Is it a male? Yes
Is he Mum and Dad's age? Yes
Is he a teacher at school? No
Has he been to our house? Yes

There are bound to be a few questions that come up for which the chooser doesn't know the precise answer, so they can be allowed to give an approximate answer sometimes.

✱ Variation

Branch out into pop stars, sports and movie stars, or even have a game based on cartoon characters.

What Am I?

A game very similar to Who Am I? but this time use things instead of people.

A player chooses a real-life object and the rest have to guess what it is by asking a series of questions for which the answer is either "yes" or "no". Unlike the previous game, this version demands a much more detailed level of questioning, because "the thing" could be a bicycle, a hockey pitch, an aircraft carrier or a chicken nugget.

✱ Variation

Instead of choosing an object, choose an animal, fish, bird or insect. Or how about a plant of some kind? There is a similar sort of game known as Hidden In My Room. The first player secretly chooses an object then says, "Hidden in my room is something that is small..." or any adjective that describes the mystery object, such as "small", "furry", "smelly", or "black".

It would be a really lucky guess to hit on the right answer in one, so the players then get another chance when the chooser adds another description.

"Hidden in my room is something that is small and circular" and if no one guesses, the chooser keeps on adding clues until it is patently obvious what it is.

You can allow all sorts of things to be hidden in a bedroom that wouldn't normally fit, all the way from a tractor to a nuclear power station.

The Next Car Will Be ...

This is a game for wandering country roads, or winding mountain roads. Or just not very busy roads.

Players guess the colour of the next car to come past them in the opposite direction – white, green, grey, red, blue, etc. – everyone with their own separate colour. There's a point for each correct guess. Set a mileage on the car's speedometer to determine the finishing line.

✱ Variation

Instead of using colours, you could pick types of vehicle that are going to come round the bend towards you.

Because cars are going to be the most common vehicles you can give higher points to other vehicles.

Trucks 2 points

Pick-ups 2 points

MPVs 3 points

Vans 3 points

Motorbikes 5 points

Car with trailer 5 points

Tractor 12 points

Police car 20 points

Abstract Questions

It's a line of questioning you often see posed in magazine interviews when a celebrity is asked, "If you were a car, what kind of car would you be?"

It's meant to draw out a lighthearted or wacky response – for cars you can be fast and sporty or big and practical or luxurious and graceful.

One player has to choose a person who they know very well. The other players must also know this person well and they have to guess who it is by asking a series of abstract questions. For example:

If this person was a tree, what would it be?
If this person was an animal, what would it be?
If this person was a kind of weather, what would it be?
If this person was an emotion, what would it be?
If this person was a piece of clothing, what would it be?

Questions continue until someone guesses the right answer.

Playing Tip

Before you start it's a good idea to limit your choices to a specific area, such as celebrities, fictional characters, people you know, etc.

To prevent the guessers getting sidetracked by misleading answers, the person answering can dodge the occasional question for which there is no obvious answer.

Old Maid

Traditionally no one wanted to be the 'Old Maid', which is possibly where this particular name for a popular 19th century card game comes from. Variations are played all over the world including Japan, Turkey, Brazil and Egypt.

What do you need?
· 2–8 players.
· One pack of cards.

Play time!

20 mins

Playing the game
First, take all the Queens out of the pack, apart from the Queen of Spades (she is the Old Maid), then choose a dealer who deals the cards, one at a time, as evenly as possible to all the players.

First the players must look at their cards and take out all the pairs (cards of the same rank), putting them face up on the table in front of them.

The dealer then offers his hand, face down, to the player on his or her left, and that player picks a card. If this card matches one in his or her hand, the pair can be discarded; if not he or she must keep the card. Play continues in a clockwise direction until there are no more pairs and the only card left is the Old Maid.

This game is not so much about winning as losing – the player left holding the Old Maid is the loser.

Top Ten
The Car's the Star!

If you took these famous cars out of their hit movies or TV series then they just wouldn't be the same. Try naming the famous cars out loud and see if your passengers know what film or TV series they were from. There's a few in there for the car-mad dads too!

1 DeLorean – Back to the Future

2 Volkswagen Beetle – Herbie Goes Bananas

3 Ecto-1 – Ghostbusters

4 KITT – Knight Rider

5 Lightning McQueen – Cars

6 General Lee – Dukes of Hazzard

7 Batmobile – Batman

8 Ford Torneo – Starsky and Hutch

9 The Mystery Machine – Scooby Doo

10 Mach 5 Van – The A-Team

Top Ten
Amazing Car Facts!

Unbelievable but true facts to tell the children — in case they are starting to get bored or fall asleep.

1. The New York City Police Department used bicycles to pursue speeding motorists in 1898.

2. In 1916, 55 per cent of the cars in the world were Model T Fords, a record that has never been beaten.

3. Most American car horns beep in the key of F.

4. The automobile is the most recycled consumer product in the world today.

5. An airbag takes only 40 milliseconds to inflate after an accident.

6. Mary Anderson patented the first windshield wiper in 1905.

7. On average a human being spends two weeks of their life waiting for traffic lights to change.

8. California has issued at least six driver's licenses to people named Jesus Christ.

9. The London motor show began in November 1895. The show consisted of five cars in a field, and only 500 people turned up.

10. The onboard computer in a modern car is more powerful than the one used to send the Apollo astronauts to the moon.

Waving Chicken

This is a game for long, empty roads with few cars about. It was told to me by someone who travelled a lot in Australia, where in the more remote parts, passing another car is a real event.

Because the most obvious "waver" is the person in the passenger seat, they have to wave on instruction from other people in the car. As another car approaches, a decision has to be made – do we wave or do we chicken out of waving?

If you wave and you get a wave back, that's a point. If you wave and you don't get a wave back, that's a minus point. If you decide not to wave and you don't get a wave, that's also a point.

But if you decide not to wave and the other car waves at you first, then that's the ultimate failure – two minus points!

The skill is working out what kind of car is coming towards you and whether the occupants of that kind of car are likely to wave or not.

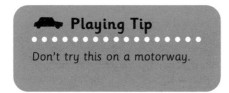

Playing Tip

Don't try this on a motorway.

Quietest in the Car

While a lot of the other car games challenge and excite the occupants of the back seats, this is one that calms everything down. This is often a great way to get younger children off to sleep. Our five-year-old daughter not only keeps very quiet, she also keeps very still and frequently drops off to sleep trying her hardest to win.

From the moment the signal is given everyone has to be as quiet as possible. The winner is the one who keeps quietest for the longest time.

These things are not allowed:

Humming
Coughing loudly
Distracting fellow competitors
Tickling other competitors

Playing Tip

If it's night time, make sure everyone's been to the bathroom, just in case of accidents...

Go Fish

The object of this game is to collect the most sets of four cards of the same rank. Don't be the one left with an empty net!

What do you need?

Play time!
30 mins

- 2–6 players, although it is best with 3–6.
- One pack of cards.

Playing the game

When playing with more than two the dealer deals five cards to each player; two players get seven cards each.

The first thing to do is to inspect your cards and then choose someone to start. This person then asks another player by name for a particular rank of card, e.g. Fives (they must already hold a card of the same rank). If the second player has any cards of this rank they must give them all to the first player. If not, they say 'Go fish', and the first player must take the top card from the draw pile. If the card drawn is the same rank as the one requested they must show it to the other players and they get another turn. If not, they must keep the card and play moves to the person that said 'Go fish'.

When you collect a set of four you must show them to the other players and put them face down on the table in front of you.

The first person with no cards left in their hand is the winner, or, if the draw pile runs out, then the winner is the person with the most sets of four.

☞ **Handy Hint**
• •
Make sure you take note of who is collecting which cards — then you can be cunning and try to steal their catch when it is your turn!

Mimes

There's more acting required in the mime game. One player has to act out an action, such as cleaning teeth, or sending an email, or taking a photograph, and the other players have to guess what it is.

Here are some ideas to get you going:

Cleaning shoes
Using the phone
Throwing a basketball
Putting on a coat
Painting a wall
Eating a banana

Using the microwave
Flying a kite
Writing a letter (don't forget the envelope and stamp)
Putting on sunglasses
Riding a motorbike

✳ Variation

Be an animal – this one can have the car in fits of laughter (certainly my meerkat had such an uproarious reaction we had to stop the vehicle once, not because it was a great impression, either, the driver just couldn't stop laughing).

Without telling the rest of the car what they are, players have to mime popular, distinctive animals, from moles to meerkats, from kangaroos to koalas

Importantly, players are not allowed to use any sound effects whatsoever. They can use their hands, for instance; to act out a cat licking its paws and cleaning its fur, or to show how big their ears are.

Car Poetry

Have a go at creating some car poetry on the move. If it's just five lines then you won't have to write the good ones down to remember them. One we created is published below.

Limericks are great fun and you can build them up slowly line by line. For example:

A beautiful princess called Hetty
Had fallen in love with spaghetti
She loved it so much
She loved even the touch
But the mess on her dress wasn't pretty

Each player can suggest a line of the limerick, or alternatively, build it up line by line together, agreeing which is the best next line as it is constructed, before moving onto the next one.

" Jokes We Used To Tell "

What happens when a frog's car breaks down?

It gets toad away!

✳ Variation

A more artistic form of poetry can be Five-Senses Poetry or Five-Colour Poetry. With Five-Senses Poetry, each line is about a different sense – touch, sight, sound, smell, and taste, all relating to the same subject.

The sight of my dog makes me happy
The smell of my dog is so doggy
The touch of my dog is furry and wet
The sound of my dog is woof, woof woof
But the taste of my dog is NEVER!

With Five-Colour Poetry, each line is about a different colour.

A rose is as red as blood
The sea is as blue as my pyjamas
The grass is a green space I play on
The fire glows orangey bright
Dad's face is as black as a thunder cloud

Weird Vacations

Everyone can have fun planning a weird vacation with this nonsense game. Players have to make up a sentence about where they're going on holiday, who they're going with and what they're going to do when they get there. The only limiting factor is they all have to begin with the same letter.

The destination, the person (or thing) they're going with and their activity must begin with the same letter. For example:

I'm off to Paris with a parrot to pick poppies.
I'm off to Iceland with an iguana to idle about in an igloo.
I'm off to Zanzibar with Zoe to zoom around a zoo.

🚗 Playing Tip

If you allow names to be used, limit players to people they know in real life.

" Jokes We Used To Tell "

What do monsters make with cars?

Traffic jam!

When I Went on Holiday ...

This is a favourite old game that people know in many different forms. Basically, it's all about remembering a long list. Or, if you're bad at it, forgetting a short one.

A player starts with the sentence: "When I went on holiday I remembered to pack ... a toothbrush."

The next player could add, for example, toothpaste. So they say: "When I went on holiday I remembered to pack a toothbrush and some toothpaste."

The next player adds another item to the list. "When I went on holiday I remembered to pack a toothbrush, some toothpaste, and my pet iguana called Alfonse." Gradually, the list grows until someone is bound to get the sequence wrong.

And then they're out.

✱ Variation

Personalize it with 'Coming back from _____ I saw ...' and make players add things they really have seen or visited during the trip.

Quiz Time
Entertainment

Many of us spend far more time at the cinema and watching television than we might care to admit, but it means we know a fair amount about popular culture.

 Betty Draper is the wife, and Peggy Olsen is the advertising executive, from which acclaimed television series?

2 'As far back as I can remember, I always wanted to be a gangster.' Ray Liotta said this in which film from 1990?

3 'You Give Love a Bad Name' and 'Livin' on a Prayer' were early hits for which band?

4 What are the surnames of Romeo and Juliet?

5 'Who loves ya, baby' was a catchphrase of which 1970s lollipop-sucking detective?

6 Who played Maximus Decimus Meridius in a 2000 Ridley Scott film?

7 What was Elvis Presley's middle name?

8 Despite the legend, in which film is 'Play it again, Sam' never actually said?

9 First performed in 1918, who composed The Planets suite?

10 In 2009, which band released the album 'West Ryder Pauper Lunatic Asylum'?

Check the answers on pages 190-191.

Opposites

A word game to challenge players' vocabulary and also their understanding of the meaning of words.

One person says a word, then the other has to find the antonym or opposite. Everyone starts with ten points and you lose a point for each time you can't find an opposite. The winner is the last one left in.

Happy/Sad

Brave/Cowardly

Strong/Weak

Loud/Quiet

Positive/Negative

Big/Small

Massive/Minute

Smelly/Odourless

Hard/Easy

Brilliant/Dull

Love/Hate

Narrow/Wide

Good/Bad

Ugly/Handsome

Tall/Short

Playing Tip

Don't let players get away with adding "un" on the front of words.

Backwards Spelling

Another great game to teach word awareness. One player thinks of a word, then, without revealing what it is, begins to spell it out loud. Except they start with the last letter first and proceed to spell the word backwards.

The other players in the car have to work out what the word is going to be. The first person to guess and shout out correctly wins the next go.

So car becomes: R-A-C
Fun becomes: N-U-F
Cloud becomes: D-U-O-L-C
Games becomes: S-E-M-A-G

Playing Tip

Start with three- or four-letter words to get into the swing of things. To help players guess the words early, you can limit the subject area to particular themes – such as animals, plants or means of transport.

The Janitor's Dog

The janitor's dog is an Awful dog.
The janitor's dog is an Awesome dog.
The janitor's dog is an Amiable dog.
The janitor's dog is an Aggressive dog.

For this game you have to find an adjective beginning with a certain letter. In this case we've used the letter "A", but it might just as well be the letter "C" or "D" (but probably not "X" or "Z").

Players take it in turn to find an adjective for the dog beginning with the letter "A", until someone repeats an adjective or gets stuck. That person is then out and the rest move on to another letter. The last person standing is the winner.

> ## ✻ Variation
>
> It's so easy to personalize this game. It doesn't have to be the janitor's dog or the farmer's horse; it could be your aunt's bathrobe or the mayor's tree.
>
> Also, to make things a little more specific, you can choose positive adjectives or negative adjectives or even energetic adjectives.

Letter Word Tag

You can play this game with all kinds of different word categories or themes. Someone decides the category, for example, "Geography". The first player picks a word such as "Caribbean" and then the second player has to name a geography-related word starting with the end letter of that word.

In this example it's the letter N, so it could be Namibia or Nova Scotia or Norway or New Orleans.

The following player has to quickly think up a destination beginning with the last letter of Namibia, and so on until someone becomes stuck and is bonged out. Start everyone off with ten points and deduct a point every time they get "bonged".

✳ Variation

How about three-letter word tag and four-letter word tag, but on any subject you like.

Knock-out Whist

Also known as Trumps this is an easy family game and is good for teaching children the idea of 'tricks'.

What do you need?

- 2–7 players.
- One pack of cards.

Play time!

15 mins

Playing the game

Choose a dealer who must then deal seven cards to each player in a clockwise direction. They must then turn over the top card of the remaining cards to indicate which suit is 'trumps'. Cards are ranked with Ace as the highest card and so on down to One, which is the lowest.

The player to the dealer's left starts and plays a card they think will win that round. In turn the other players must try and beat that card, either by playing a higher card from the same suit, or if they have no cards from that suit, by playing a 'trump' card. The winner of each trick gets to start the next one and so on until all the cards from that round have been used. Any player that wins no tricks in a round is 'knocked out' and is dealt no more cards.

In the next round each player is given six cards, the winner of the most tricks from the last round gets to choose the 'trump' suit and begins the round. If there is a tie the players can cut cards and the one with the higher card gets to choose trumps. Play continues like this with players being dealt one card less each round.

Winner takes all

The last player left in at the end is the winner.

DropOut

This is a crafty word construction game that involves a bit of bluffing.

Like the never-ending sentence game, the idea is not to finish a word off. One player starts off with the first letter of a word, the second player adds a second letter, and so on – everyone who adds a letter must have an end word in mind, though they don't have to reveal it unless challenged. The letter they add mustn't complete a word.

For example:

Player 1: "H"

Player 2: "O" – they're thinking of the word "home"

Player 3: "S" – they're thinking of the word "host" (and "hos" isn't a word)

Player 4: "P" – they're thinking of the word "hospital" (and "hosp" isn't a word)

Player 1: "I" – they're thinking of the word "hospice or hospital" (and "hospi" isn't a word)

Player 2: "T" – they're thinking of the word "hospital" too and realize that Player 4 is going to get stuck with the last letter.

Player 3: "A" – they also realize that Player 4 is stuck with the word "hospital".

Player 4: "L" – they lose.

Player 4 collects the letter "D" for losing a round, the next time they lose it's the letter "R", then "O", then "P" until Player 4 becomes a DropOut and leaves the game.

If you add a letter you have to have an end word in mind. If the other players think that you don't they can challenge you. If you can't come up with an end word, then you receive a letter from DropOut. Alternatively, if someone challenges you about your end word and you have got a legitimate word in mind, then they collect a letter from DropOut.

" Jokes We Used To Tell "

What kind of ears do trains have?

Engineers (engine ears)!

Top Ten
Pioneers of Motoring!

When the car was first invented it changed how the whole world travelled. And it brought everybody who lived miles away that little bit nearer — even in-laws! These facts are great for guessing games and, who knows, you may all end up learning something too!

1. The first car radio was invented in 1929.

2. The first cars had levers instead of steering wheels

3. The first car to be offered for sale was the Benz in 1887.

4. The first speeding ticket was issued in 1902.

5. The first ever grand prix motor race was held in France in 1906.

6. The first Monaco Grand Prix was in 1929.

7. The first fuel gauge appeared on cars in 1922. Up until then it was guesswork!

8. The American car maker Buick introduced the first electric turn signals in 1938 – up until then drivers had to signal with their hands.

9. The first ever land speed record was set on December 18 1898, when a French race car driver reached a dizzying speed of 39mph in an electric car.

10. The first self-propelled car was invented by Nicolas Cugnot in 1769.

Classic Indoor Games

• • • • • • • • • • •

Some of the best games are played indoors with the whole family gathered around. Charades is a classic game that all ages can enjoy together (but remember younger players may not know your favourite movie from the 1980s) and Consequences always ends with heaps of laughter. Braver players can go for a game of Are You There, Moriarty?, just don't swing too hard!

Mummies

Tell the boys not to worry; no dolls are required for this game, just toilet roll and lots of laughter.

Stuff to Find

- An even number of players.
- A roll of toilet paper for each pair.

play time!

10 mins

House Rules

Divide the players into pairs and give each team a roll of toilet paper. One member of the team then has three minutes to wrap their partner up in paper from head to foot so that they look like an Egyptian mummy. When the time is up, the team with the best mummy is the winner.

☞ Playing Tip

When the game is finished, please remember to recycle your toilet paper or, better still, wind it up and keep it for wiping noses or cleaning up mess.

Light and Shade

This game reminds me of shadow theatre. How will you hide your true identity from the audience?

Stuff to Find

- Six or more players.
- A white sheet.
- A lamp or torch.

Play time!

20 mins

House Rules

Hang the sheet across the room – a length of washing line and clothes pegs is probably the best way – and set up a lamp or shine a torch behind it.

Divide the players into two teams; members of the first team walk behind the sheet one at a time so their shadows are visible to the opposing team. This team then tries to guess the identity of the person behind the sheet – who is doing their best to disguise their silhouette. The team guessing gets two attempts per shadow and scores a point for each correct guess. Then the other team has their turn.

At the end of the game, the team with the most points wins.

Blindfold Drawing

However talented you are at drawing, a blindfold creates a level playing field where art is concerned – as well as some hilarious pictures.

Stuff to Find

Play time!

10 mins

- Two or more players.
- A blindfold, some paper and a pencil for each player.

House Rules

Make sure all the players have a piece of paper and a pencil and are securely blindfolded. Then tell them what to draw. For example, start with their house, then ask them to add some trees in the garden, a car, some people, and so on – you can be as inventive as you like.

When the pictures are finished, everyone removes their blindfolds to see what they have drawn. There are no winners here – the laughter is the prize.

" Jokes We Used To Tell "

What happened when the chicken slept under her car?

She woke up oily next morning!

Deadpan

I love thinking of what to do next for this game. Most of the time, though, I only have to look as if I am going to tickle someone and my kids collapse into giggles.

Stuff to Find

* Four or more players.

Play time!

10 mins

House Rules

Everyone must sit on the floor in a circle as close together as possible. Choose a leader and then the game can start.

The leader nudges the person on their left and so on around the circle. When the nudge comes back to the leader, they then tweak the ear of the person on their left, and so on around the circle as before. Next time the leader can pull their neighbour's nose, tickle their ear, mess up their hair – basically anything to try to make them laugh. Speed is the name of the game. Anyone who even smiles – let alone giggles or laughs – is disqualified and must leave the circle.

Feelers

I used to play this at parties when I was young: anything slimy would have me running for the door!

Stuff to Find

- Three or more players.
- A pencil and some paper for each player.
- A pillowcase filled with assorted objects – 10 should be enough.

Play time!

20 mins

House Rules

Fill a pillowcase with an assortment of objects. The best ones to choose are items that could be mistaken for something else – for example, a grapefruit could also be a large orange, or a coin could be mistaken for another of a different value, etc.

Pass the pillowcase around, allowing each player 30 seconds to have a good feel before writing down as many of the objects they think they can identify. The player with the most accurate list is the winner.

" Things Grandpas Say "

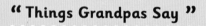

The grass is always greener on the other side of the fence.

Noises Off

You can let your imagination run away with you when preparing for this game – the more inventive the better, and the more fun everyone will have.

Play time!

15 mins

Stuff to Find

- Three or more players.
- Some paper and a pencil for each player.
- Everything you need to make some confusing and outrageous noises.

House Rules

This game is probably better if it is organised in advance – then you can get together a whole range of unusual sounds.

The person making the noises must go behind a door or screen so they cannot be seen by the other players. They then make a succession of sounds that the other players have to guess and write down. The player that recognises the most sounds is the winner.

✱ Noisy Suggestions

Gargling

Kissing

Chalk on a blackboard

Finger clicking

Dropping a pin

Cracking an egg

Bouncing a ball

Squeak Piggy Squeak!

Remember, the sillier the squeak, the harder it is for the farmer to guess who you are!

Stuff to Find

- Five or more players.
- A blindfold and a cushion.

Play time!

20 mins

House Rules

Choose one player to be the 'farmer' and the others are the 'piggies'. The piggies sit down in a circle while the farmer is blindfolded and stands in the middle. Spin the farmer three times; they must then find their way, with their cushion, to one of the piggies and sit on their lap without touching the piggy with their hands. The farmer now says 'Squeak Piggy Squeak'; the chosen piggy must squeak and the farmer guesses the name of the player they are sitting on. If the farmer guesses correctly, the piggy is the farmer for the next round. If the farmer gets it wrong, then they stay to be spun again. It is a good idea for the piggies to change places before the next round begins.

Top Ten
Excuses For Not Doing Homework

We've all forgotten to do homework before. The question is, did you own up ... or did you tell a little lie?

1 The dog ate it.

2 I couldn't find the answers anywhere.

3 The house was cold so we had to set fire to it to keep warm.

4 Homework? I thought you were joking.

5 I was abducted by aliens and they only brought me back this morning.

6 It was in my backpack this morning, someone must have stolen it.

7 It fell out of my bag as I helped an old lady across the road.

8 My dad accidentally put it in his briefcase.

9 I had better things to do.

10 I didn't want to make the rest of the class look bad by doing so well.

Murder in the Dark

Played in the dark, this detective game is especially atmospheric. It is also good practice for anyone who has always longed to be Hercule Poirot for the evening.

Stuff to Find

- Six or more players.
- Pack of cards, or some paper, a pencil and a bowl or hat, and a house with lots of hiding places!

House Rules

If you are playing with a pack of cards, find the following: Ace, Jack, Queen, King and number cards for the remaining players. Give a card to each person. The player with the Ace is the murderer and the person holding the Jack is the detective. The King becomes the detective if the Jack is murdered, and the Queen becomes the detective if both the Jack and King are murdered.

If you are playing with pencil and paper, tear the paper into as many pieces as there are players. Mark a cross on one piece and a circle on another. The rest of the pieces stay blank. Fold up the paper slips and put them in a hat or bowl. Each player then picks one. The player that chooses the cross is the murderer and the person with the circle is the detective.

Before the game starts, the detective identifies him- or herself. Turn off the lights, and everyone find a place to hide. The murderer then finds a 'victim', touches them on the shoulder and whispers 'You're dead'. The player falls to the floor while letting out a bloodcurdling scream as the murderer creeps away.

When the players hear the scream, they must stay where they are. The detective then needs to go to the crime scene and switch on the lights, noting where everyone is. Now the detective calls everyone into the main room and asks the suspects a series of questions. Those that are innocent must tell the truth but the murderer can lie unless they are asked directly whether or not they are guilty. Once all the evidence has been collected, the detective then has two chances to guess the identity of the murderer.

" Jokes We Used To Tell "

A man was caught for speeding and went before the judge. The judge said, "What will you take: 30 days or £30?" The man thought about it for a minute and then replied, "I think I'll take the money."

I Have Never

I Have Never – had a filling in my adult teeth. I wonder how many people reading this can say that...

Stuff to Find

* Three or more players.

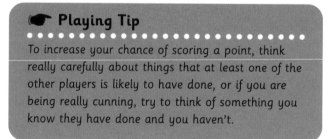

Play time!

15
mins

House Rules

Each player takes it in turn to declare something that they have never done. For example, you might say, 'I have never had a school meal'. If you turn out to be the only person that has never had a school meal, then you score a point, and the first person to gain three points wins the game.

☞ Playing Tip

To increase your chance of scoring a point, think really carefully about things that at least one of the other players is likely to have done, or if you are being really cunning, try to think of something you know they have done and you haven't.

Wink Murder

I was never very good at screaming (see Murder in the Dark, pages 140-141), so pretending to die in an over-dramatic way was much more my thing.

Stuff to Find
- Four or more players.
- A pack of cards.

Play time!

15 mins

House Rules
Draw as many cards from the pack as there are players – one of these cards must be the Ace of Spades. Lay the cards on the table, and ask each player to pick a card, keeping its identity secret. The person with the Ace of Spades is the 'murderer'.

Sit everyone in a circle. Once the murderer has caught someone's eye, they wink in their direction and this player must slump forward and 'die'. The idea is for the murderer to kill everyone without their identity being discovered. If any of the players spot the murderer, then the game begins again.

> ## " Jokes We Used To Tell "
> ·
> Why do cows have bells?
>
> **Because their horns don't work**

In the Manner of the Word

Also known as Adverbs, this game dates from the nineteenth century, and is a great way to teach a valuable grammatical tool without anyone noticing or using the words 'It's not fair'!

Stuff to Find

• Four or more people.

Play time!
5 mins per round

House Rules

There are two versions of this game. In either version, if you are able to guess the adverb you win the round, but with this game no one really cares.

Individuals

One person leaves the room and those remaining choose an adverb – for example, 'aggressively', 'wearily', 'excitedly', and so on. When the choice has been made, the person is called back into the room and they have to guess what the adverb is. They can do this either by asking questions that the other players have to answer 'in the manner of the word', or they can ask the player to act out an everyday situation, such as cleaning the windows or driving a car, also 'in the manner of the word'.

Pairs

In this version, two people go out of the room to think of an adverb. When they return, the others have to guess what it is by giving the pair situations to act out – you've guessed it – 'in the manner of the word'. Perhaps milking a cow, washing their hair, cutting the grass, etc.

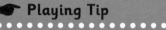

Playing Tip

• More common adverbs are easier for younger players to manage.
• The second version is better suited to players with more inhibitions – they get to share the embarrassment!

" Things Mums Say "

Do as I say, not as I do.

Charades

Charades is already a great favourite in my house. However, I am getting slightly weary of having to guess 'The Princess and the Frog' for the umpteenth time, and am looking forward to seeing the mime for 'Harry Potter and the Half-blood Prince' instead!

Stuff to Find

- Four or more people.

House Rules

Charades can be played in teams or as individuals. The idea is to act out the name of a well-known book, film, play, song, television programme, person or even a familiar saying, using a combination of actions and mime – speaking at any time is against the rules and will result in immediate disqualification.

- If you are playing as individuals, one person acts out their choice and everyone else must try to guess what it is. The person that guesses correctly wins a point. If no one gets it, the person acting gets the point.
- If you are playing in teams, you need to decide which team starts and within that team which member goes first. That team member acts out their choice to their own team who scores a point if they guess correctly.
- If they can't guess it then it, goes over to the other team who can score a bonus point if they can get it right.

Once you have mimed the category your choice is from, you can indicate the number of words it contains by holding up the relevant number of fingers: first word, second word, third word, etc.

Some words are easy to act out, for instance, you can point to objects or people around the room. However, there are some other useful actions that can help with other words:

☞ Categories

Book put your hands together and open them like a book.

Film pretend to be winding an old-fashioned movie camera.

Play put your hands together in front of you and move them downwards and apart to indicate curtains in a theatre.

Song bring a hand to your open mouth and then move it away to indicate sound.

Television programme draw a square in the air using two hands.

Saying use the index and middle finger of each hand to indicate quotation marks.

☞ Useful Actions

Small word holding your thumb and index finger a short distance apart indicates a small word. The other players must then shout out common small words, 'in', 'of', 'at', 'on', 'to', 'a', and you point to the first person to get it right.

The is indicated by making a letter 'T' with the index fingers of both hands.

Sounds like pinching your ear lobe is a way of showing that the word you want the players to guess 'sounds like' a word that is easier to act out.

Syllables you can also break a word up into syllables to make it easier to create the word. The action for this is to place the relevant number of fingers on the underside of your opposite forearm. For instance, if you had decided on the book 'To Kill a Mockingbird', you could break the last word up into three syllables.

Whole thing you can choose to act out the whole title; the action for this is to draw a circle in the air with both arms.

Dumb Crambo

The spoken version of this game – Crambo – is an old rhyming game that has been played for hundreds of years.

Play time!
15 mins per round

Stuff to Find
• Six or more people.

House Rules
Divide the players into two teams. One team leaves the room while the other thinks of a word. The first team is called back and are not told the word but a word that rhymes with it (for example, if the word is 'bite', the word they give to the opposing team might be 'night').

The team think of three words that rhyme with 'night' that could be the correct answer. When they return to the room they must act out their guesses one by one. When the guesses are incorrect, the first team has the chance to boo and hiss to show their displeasure, but, if the answer is right, then this must be greeted with a great round of applause.

✳ Variation

In the spoken version of this game, the team guessing can ask questions to find out what the word is. As above, they are given a word that rhymes with the chosen word and have three chances to guess correctly, but must ask indirect questions, for example:
• Is it something you turn on using a switch [a light – incorrect]?
• Is it something you might get from a mosquito [a bite – correct]?

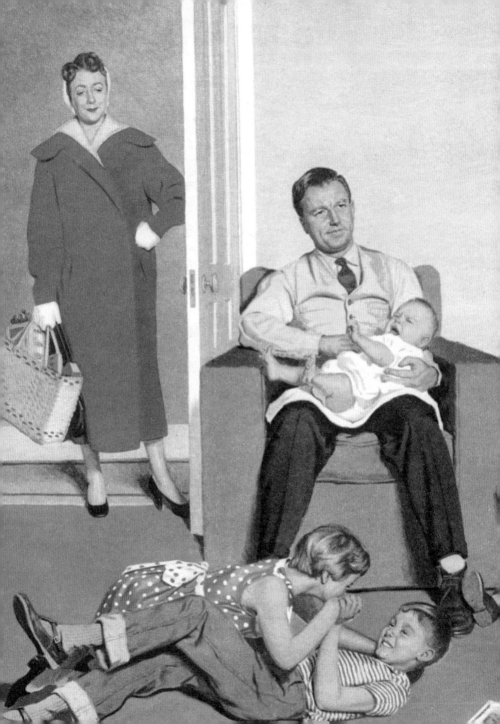

Top Ten
Boys' Names of the 1950s and Now

Even though many of the most popular boys' names have remained the same over the years, try and recall when you last heard a boy being called his actual name? Boys much prefer calling each other nicknames. So, instead of James, Oliver, Thomas and William you get Jimmy, Olly, Tommy and Billy instead!

1950	Now
1 James	Oliver (Olly)
2 Robert	Jack (Jacky)
3 John	Harry ('Arry)
4 Michael	Alfie (Alf)
5 David	Joshua (Josh)
6 William	Thomas (Tommy)
7 Richard	Charles (Charlie)
8 Thomas	William (Billy)
9 Charles	James (Jimmy)
10 Stephen	Daniel (Danny)

(Office of National Statistics, 2010)

Consequences

Guaranteed to produce both hysterical laughter and some of the most unlikely couples since Arthur Miller and Marilyn Monroe, this game works for all age groups and across generations.

Stuff to Find

- Two or more people.
- A pencil to share or one each and lots of paper – once you start you'll want to keep going!

Play time!

15 mins

House Rules

The aim of this game is to produce a hilarious short story by taking turns to write the different stages of the story without the other players knowing what you have written.

Choose someone to start and, using one piece of paper, begin the story by writing at the top. Once you have finished, you must fold the paper over so what is written cannot be seen, and pass it to the next player.

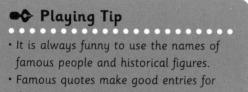

●← Playing Tip

- It is always funny to use the names of famous people and historical figures.
- Famous quotes make good entries for 'he said' and 'she said'.

A number of different versions of the story formula exist but most include the following:

1. [Boy's name] met
2. [Girl's name] at
3. [Where they met]
4. He did [what he did]
5. She did [what she did]
6. He said [what he said to her]
7. She said [what she said to him]
8. And the consequence was [describe the consequence]
9. And the world said [what the world said].

✱ Variation

Alternatively, and this works better with a larger group of people, you can play a version where everyone has a piece of paper and a pencil and starts at the beginning. Once the first stage has been written, pass the paper to the player on your right.

Beetle

This game is down to the luck of the dice, and you don't need to be a great artist to play so everyone can join in.

Stuff to Find

- Between two and eight people.
- One dice and a piece of paper and a pencil for each player.

Play time!

10 mins

House Rules

The parts of the beetle are numbered to correspond with the numbers on the dice:

- 1 = body
- 2 = head
- 3 = tail
- 4 = eyes
- 5 = feelers
- 6 = legs

Taking it in turns, the object of the game is to throw the dice until you have a complete beetle. A finished beetle must have a body, a head, a tail, two eyes, two feelers and six legs.

Remember, you must throw a one (for a body) to start – if you don't, play passes to your left. You can't add eyes or feelers until you have a head (a two).

The first player to complete a beetle shouts 'Beetle' and wins the game.

Noughts and Crosses

Known in the US as Tic-tac-toe, this is a quick, addictive and competitive game.

Stuff to Find

Play time!

1–3 mins

- Two players.
- Some paper and a pencil.

House Rules

Draw a simple four-line grid creating nine spaces (three rows of three). One player is 'X' and the other 'O'. Traditionally the person who is 'X' goes first but that is up to you!

The first player places their mark in one space in the grid, then the second player does the same. The aim of the game is to get three of your marks in a row, either horizontally, vertically or diagonally. The player that succeeds in doing this is the winner.

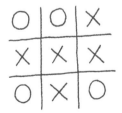

Boxes

A great game of skill and strategy, Boxes is a good way to pass the time wherever you are. It can be surprisingly difficult, though, so don't get too frustrated and watch out for sibling arguments!

Stuff to Find

- Two people.
- Some paper and pens of two different colours to avoid disagreements.

Play time!

10 mins

House Rules

Mark out a grid using the same number of dots horizontally and vertically – 10 in each direction is about right for a 10-minute game.

Each using a different colour, you and your partner must take it in turns to draw a line between any two dots on the grid, in an attempt to make a box. When you complete a box, you can mark it with your initial and then draw another line and so on. If the line encloses another box you mark it too.

When all the boxes have been completed, the game is over and you must count up your boxes to see who has the most – that person is the winner.

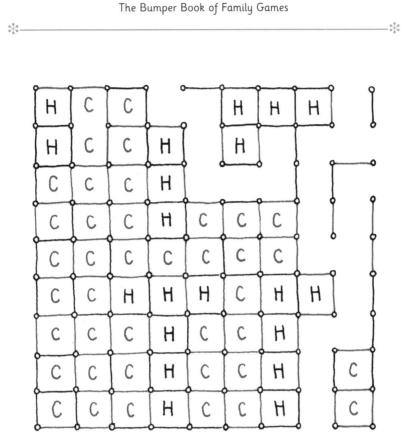

✱ Variation

For a change, you can always play the game with the reverse approach – so the person with the fewest boxes wins.

Battleships

Your grandad will prefer the traditional version of this game but you can choose any vessels you like – starships, pirate ships, army vehicles – it's up to you.

Stuff to Find

Play time!

15 mins

- Two players.
- A pencil and some paper.

House Rules

Each player needs to draw two grids 10 squares by 10 squares, numbered from one to 10 down the left-hand side and from A to J across the top. One grid is for the home fleet and the other is for the enemy fleet. Each player's fleet consists of:

- One battleship (four squares marked with a 'B')
- Two cruisers (three squares each marked with a 'C')
- Three destroyers (two squares each marked with a 'D')
- Four submarines (one square marked with an 'S').

Mark your ships on your home fleet grid. The squares that make up each ship must touch one another horizontally, vertically or diagonally and no two ships should touch.

Toss a coin to decide who starts and then the players take turns to try to hit the enemy fleet. You do this by calling out the reference for the square (for example, 'C6', 'A8'). All direct hits must be declared by the enemy and the type of vessel given honestly. You can mark your hits and misses on your enemy fleet grid and plot your progress.

The winner is the first player to destroy the enemy fleet.

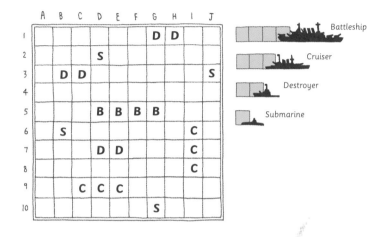

" Jokes We Used To Tell "

What driver doesn't have a license?

A screw driver!

Quiz Time
Geography

Geography got a bad rap when I was at school: the teachers wore brown suits, we didn't care what an ox-bow lake was, and what was a tertiary industry? However, to even the score, here are some really good questions on geography and travel – how many do you know?

 Which island group includes Ibiza, Menorca and Majorca?

2 The ancient city of Machu Picchu
is in which country?

3 Dulles International Airport
serves which American city?

4 On which river are the Victoria Falls found?

5 Which landlocked sea is 422m (1385ft)
below sea level?

6 What is created when the loop of a
meander of a river is cut off and the river
diverted on a different course?

7 Of which republic are English, Malay, Mandarin
Chinese and Tamil the four official languages?

8 Which country's flag includes a cedar tree?

9 Mauritius is found in which ocean?

10 Who developed the most-used projection
for maps of the world in 1569?

Check the answers on pages 190-191.

Twenty Questions

Also known as 'Animal, Vegetable or Mineral?' this game is an old favourite. It is also a good way to make something educational feel like fun.

Stuff to Find
- Three or more people.

House Rules
In the traditional version, one player thinks of an object or concept and tells the others what category it is.

The players are allowed 20 questions that require Yes or No answers designed to limit the field and eventually close in on the word. You can make a direct challenge, 'Is it XX?', but, if you get the answer wrong, you are out of that round. The first player to guess correctly gets to choose the next word but, if no one guesses the answer the person who chose the word is the winner for that round and can choose again.

Categories
- **Animal** includes animal products (food types, fabrics, etc.) as well as people and animals.
- **Vegetable** everything organic that is not related to animals.
- **Mineral** anything that is not alive.
- **Abstract** something non-material.
- **A mixture** the word includes elements of more than one of the other categories; it does help to say what the primary quality is.

✳ Variation

For a change, you can play the game the other way around: one player leaves the room and everyone else chooses a word. When they return, the person guessing gets 20 questions to try to work out the answer. This can be played as a knockout competition too: each player continues in the game until they fail to answer correctly. The last person left is the winner.

" Jokes We Used To Tell "

What do you call a man with a tyre round his head?

Anything you like, he can't hear you!

Botticelli

This complex game used to be known as The Box, because the person questioned feels as if they are in the witness box.

Stuff to Find

- Three or more people.

House Rules

Player one thinks of a famous character – fictional or real, dead or alive. They then announce the first letter of the person's surname to the rest of the players. The players now have to think of someone whose name begins with that letter and, taking it in turns, they ask indirect questions about the famous character.

Player 1: My surname begins with 'D'.
Player 2: Do you solve mysteries?

Player one now has to think of a character whose surname begins with the same letter that answers the question. When they think of it, if it is incorrect, they tell the players it is not them and the next player asks another indirect question.

Player 1: No, I am not Scooby Doo.
Player 3: Are you famous for drawing a mouse?

If player one can't think of an answer, they tell the group. The player who asked the last question gives the answer and then asks a direct question and player one must answer with 'yes' or 'no'.

Player 1: I don't know.
Player 3: Walt Disney. Are you an actor?
Player 1: No.

Sometimes there is more than one answer to an indirect question, and player one may respond with one of the other answers.

Player 4: Are you a cartoon duck?
Player 1: No, I am not Daffy Duck.

But if this is a direct question they must confirm their identity.

Player 1: Yes, I am Donald Duck.

If no one guesses in 20 minutes, player one wins and announces their identity. If another player guesses, then that player becomes player one in the next round.

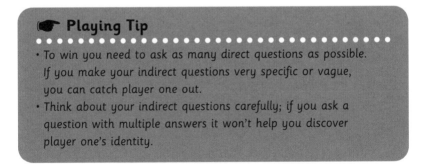

☞ Playing Tip

• To win you need to ask as many direct questions as possible. If you make your indirect questions very specific or vague, you can catch player one out.
• Think about your indirect questions carefully; if you ask a question with multiple answers it won't help you discover player one's identity.

Buzz, Fizz, Fizz-Buzz

These three closely related games involve substituting words for numbers. As well as being fun, they can help younger ones learn their times-tables – and can help older players revise them!

Stuff to Find

- Two or more players.

Play time!

5 mins

House Rules

All three games begin in the same way. The players sit in a circle and the first person begins counting from 'one'. The faster the game is, the more fun it is – and the easier it is to make a mistake!

Buzz

In this version, every time you reach a number with a seven, or any multiple of seven, you must say 'Buzz'.

Fizz

If you are playing Fizz, you must use the word 'Fizz' when you reach a number with a five or any multiple of five.

Fizz-Buzz

Unsurprisingly, Fizz-Buzz is a combination of the two, and you must use either 'Fizz' or 'Buzz', or both at the same time (in the case of 35, 57, 70 and 75) at the appropriate time.

Any player who says a number instead of Fizzing or Buzzing, or who Fizzes when they should have Buzzed (or vice versa), is out of the game. The last player left in is the winner.

Chase the Ace

The initial bets made in this game mean the prospect of winning this game becomes even more attractive – especially if they are edible!

What do you need?

- 3 or more players.
- One pack of cards.
- Some small items to use as a stake – such as sweets, marbles or matchsticks.

Play time!

5
mins per hand

Playing the game

The dealer shuffles the cards and deals one card to each player. Each player starts with the same number of 'lives', e.g. three, and everyone puts a stake in the 'pot' that will be collected by the overall winner. The cards rank from King (high) to Ace (low).

The player to the left of the dealer goes first and looks at his or her card. They can either keep the card or swap it with the player on their left in the hope of getting a better (higher) card. The neighbouring player must accept the swap unless her or she has a King. In this case the card is shown to everyone and the player keeps the card. The dealer has the last turn and can swap their card with one from the stock pile, although if this turns out to be a King they must keep their original card.

When all the players have had their turn everyone must show their cards and whoever has the lowest card loses a life. If more than one person has a card with the lowest value they all lose a life, and players who have lost all their lives must drop out of the game.

The last person left in the game is the winner (and takes the 'pot').

The Yes/No Game

Just how hard is it not to use the words 'yes' or 'no' under pressure? Why don't you find out?

Stuff to Find

Play time!

20 mins

- Two or more players.
- A watch to time the rounds.

House Rules

For this game, one person asks questions and another person answers. The person answering must not answer 'yes' or 'no' to any questions during the two-minute round. You can also ban words like 'er' and 'um' to make it harder.

> ## " Jokes We Used To Tell "
> ●
>
> Why did the horse cross the road?
>
> **Because it was the chicken's day off!**

Taboo

This game proves yet again that doing something very simple is actually very difficult – and we all know how much children like to make their parents look silly!

Play time!

20 mins

Stuff to Find
- Three or more people.

House Rules
Choose a word that comes up frequently in conversation, such as 'and', 'the' or 'it'; once everyone has agreed on the word it becomes 'taboo'. Then one person becomes the question master and asks the other players about anything at all in an attempt to make them say the forbidden word – anyone who does so, or hesitates, is out, and the last player left is the winner.

> ## ✳ Variation
> To make the game more difficult, you can make a letter of the alphabet taboo and any word containing it is also taboo. This version is only for experienced players!

Top Ten
Knock, Knock Jokes

Everybody loves Knock Knock jokes. Even the really bad ones can be funny and have the whole car in hysterics. Take it in turn and go around the car. Whose was the worst? Here are some of my favourites that I've picked up along the way. What are yours?

1 Knock knock
Who's there?
Albert
Albert who?
Albert you don't know who this is.

2 Knock knock
Who's there?
Ivor
Ivor who?
Ivor plane to catch so I can't stop long!

3 Knock knock
Who's there?
Aladdin
Aladdin who?
Aladdin the street's just pinched your bike!

4 Knock knock
Who's there?
Colleen
Colleen who?
Colleen all police vehicles in the area!

5 Knock knock
Who's there?
Eileen
Eileen who?
Eileen'd on your car and dented it, sorry!

6 Knock knock
Who's there?
Warner
Warner who?
Warner lift, my car's outside!!

7 Knock knock
Who's there?
Noah
Noah who?
Noah good place where I can get my car fixed?

8 Knock knock
Who's there?
Isobel
Isobel who?
Isobel worth having on a bicycle?!

9 Knock knock
Who's there?
Fred
Fred who?
Fred you'll have to catch the bus 'cos I've got a flat tyre

10 Knock knock
Who's there?
Wanda
Wanda who?
Wanda buy a cheap car? It's got no wheels but...

Tiddlywinks

Elevated from a parlour game played by children to an international sport, the game of Tiddlywinks was first patented in Britain in 1888 by Joseph Assheton Fincher. This simplified version is great for playing at home.

Stuff to Find

- Two to four people.
- A set of coloured counters for each player, each consisting of six smaller 'winks' and a larger 'squidger' used to flick the 'winks'.
- A rectangular piece of felt or other non-slip fabric.
- A plastic pot.

Play time!

20 mins

House Rules

Place each set of counters in a corner of the playing mat and the plastic pot in the centre. If two people are playing, they can use two sets each; in a team game, the team members should sit diagonally opposite one another, and play moves clockwise around the mat.

A 'squidge-off' decides who goes first: each player flicks or 'squidges' one wink as close to the pot as possible. The winner gets to go first. The aim is to get all your winks into the pot (to 'pot out'). If you pot a wink, you get an extra turn. If you shoot a wink off the mat, it must be returned to its original position and you miss a turn. If one wink lands on top of another, that wink becomes 'squopped' and neither of these winks can be played.

The game ends when you reach the time limit, when a player pots out, or when there are no more playable winks. If no one pots out, you can count all the winks in the pot and the player (or team) with the most wins.

Pass the Orange

No hands are allowed for this game so it is a good thing that oranges are so resilient!

Stuff to Find

- Two teams, ideally six or more on each side.
- An orange for each team.

Play time!

15–20 mins

House Rules

Each team stands in a line and the first player in each tucks the orange under their chin. They then have to pass the orange to the next player without using their hands. When the orange reaches the end of the line, that player runs to the front of the line and the process begins again. Play continues until the first person returns to the front of the line. This team is the winner.

> **" Things Grandmas Say "**
>
> A bird in the hand is worth two in the bush.

Paper, Scissors, Stone

Great fun for all ages even young children.

Stuff to Find
- Two players.

Play time!

30 sec per round

House Rules
Both players hold out one hand in a fist and count 'One, two, three' before each making one of the three signs below at the same time:
- Paper an open hand.
- Scissors index and middle fingers used to imitate scissors.
- Stone a clenched fist.

The outcomes are as follows:
- Stone blunts scissors stone defeats scissors.
- Scissors cut paper scissors defeats paper.
- Paper covers stone paper defeats stone.

This game is usually played as a 'best of three', but, if you both make the same sign, then that round is not counted.

Duck, Duck, Goose

Children love this game so it is a good opportunity for the grown-ups to have a well-earned rest.

Stuff to Find

- Five or more players.

House Rules

The players sit in a large circle facing inwards. One player is chosen to be 'It' (or the 'Fox') and walks around the outside of the circle. As the Fox walks around, they touch each player gently on the head saying 'Duck, Duck, Duck'. At some point the Fox will say 'Goose' instead of 'Duck'. The 'Goose' must then jump up and chase the Fox around the circle. The Fox must try to get all the way back to the Goose's place without getting caught.

If the Fox gets there safely, the Goose becomes the Fox and the game starts again. If the Goose catches the Fox, the same Fox must try to catch the next Goose.

Fish Flap

This is a perfect way to make good use of all those free newspapers that come through your front door.

Stuff to Find

- Three or more players.
- Some old newspapers.
- Scissors and a pen.

Play time!

15 mins

House Rules

Draw a basic fish shape, about 30cm (12in) long, onto the front of one of the newspapers. Cut around the shape through all layers and give a fish to each player. The players will also need a few sheets from a newspaper folded into a rectangle. This needs to be rigid to flap the 'fish' along the floor.

Designate starting and finishing lines, and at the signal 'Go' the players must flap their fish to the finish. The first one to the there is the winner.

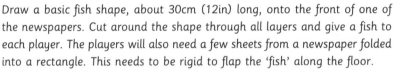

☛ **Playing Tip**

Decorating the fish means they won't get mixed up during the race.

Quiz Time
Art and Literature

Everyone has a favourite novel, and, even if we might not like art, we always have an opinion about it – that's the point. Answer these 10 questions and see how cultured you are.

1 Which American abstract artist is best known for his 'drip paintings'?

2 The Bennet family appear in which Jane Austen novel?

3 Who created the famous sculptures 'The Thinker' and 'The Kiss'?

4 Who was the father of Goneril, Regan and Cordelia?

5 How are the sisters Meg, Jo, Beth and Amy described in the title of an 1868 novel?

6 Who painted 'The Laughing Cavalier'?

Rummy

There's something exciting about holding a 'hand' of cards – I definitely felt very grown up the first time I played this game.

What do you need?

- 2–6 players.
- One pack of cards.

Play time!
10–15
mins
per
hand

Playing the game

Choose a dealer who must then deal the following numbers of cards one at a time:

- 2 players: 10 cards each
- 3–4 players: 7 cards each
- 5–6 players: 6 cards each.

When the deal is finished the stock pile is placed face down in the middle of the table and the first card is turned over and placed next to it to form the start of the discard pile.

The aim of Rummy is to get rid of all the cards in your hand. There are three ways to do this:

Melding creating a sequence (cards of the same suit in consecutive order) or set (cards of the same rank) of three of more cards. Once collected these can be laid on the table in front of you.

Laying off adding one or more cards to a meld already on the table, i.e. by adding to the beginning or end of a sequence, or adding another card of the same value to an existing set.

Hangman

This works well as a game for two slightly older children playing together, but at the moment my two play as a team against me so they can help each other out.

Stuff to Find

- Two players.
- Some paper and a pencil.

Play time!

10 mins

House Rules

The first player thinks of a word and draws a row of dashes to represent each letter of the word. The second player then needs to guess the letters in the word. If they guess a letter that does occur, the first player writes it in where it appears (this may be more than once). If the suggested letter does not appear, the first player draws one element of the hangman diagram instead.

Features of the diagram vary depending on where you learned to play this game. The version I know contained 12 elements, as seen opposite. This means you can suggest up to 11 incorrect letters before you lose the game.

The game is over when the word is completed or guessed correctly or the first player completes the hangman diagram.

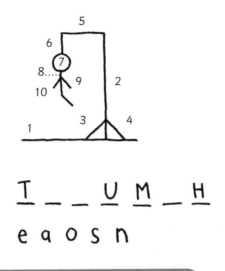

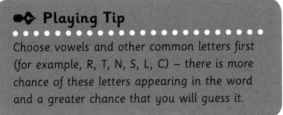

●← Playing Tip

Choose vowels and other common letters first
(for example, R, T, N, S, L, C) – there is more
chance of these letters appearing in the word
and a greater chance that you will guess it.

" Things Grandmas Say "

Don't pull that face: the wind will
change and it will stay that way.

Are You There, Moriarty?

This game was invented in the late nineteenth century when Sherlock Holmes and his nemesis Moriarty were all the rage. Make sure you have a referee – dads in particular can take games like this a bit too seriously!

Stuff to Find
- Two players, plus an audience.
- Two rolled-up newspapers.
- Two blindfolds.

Play time!

1 min per round

House Rules
Each player is blindfolded and given a rolled-up newspaper to use as a 'weapon' – make sure the newspapers are strong enough to deal an accurate blow but not rigid enough to cause an injury! Flip a coin to see who will start.

The players must then lie down on their fronts opposite one another, head to head, about 1m (3ft) apart. The starting player says, 'Are you there, Moriarty?' and, when they are ready, the other player says 'Yes'. When the first player has heard where their opponent's voice is coming from, they then attempt to hit them on the head with the newspaper.

If the first player misses, their opponent is then given the opportunity to ask, 'Are you there, Moriarty?' and have their go at scoring a hit. The game continues until one of the players succeeds in hitting the other on the head. Two new players can now join the game – or you can play 'winner stays on' if you prefer.

✱ Variation

You can also play this game standing up and holding opposite hands. Ducking and weaving will help you avoid being hit in this version.

☞ Playing Tip

To avoid being hit you can roll to one side or the other after answering 'Yes'. If you can do this quickly after speaking, you will have a definite advantage.

" Things Mums Say "

Put that down! You don't know where it's been!

Bulls and Cows

This is the predecessor of the better-known board game Mastermind, which was invented in 1971 by the wonderfully named Mordecai Meirowitz, a postmaster from Israel.

Stuff to Find

Play time!

15 mins

- Two players.
- Some paper and a pencil for each player.

House Rules

The players must decide who will be the code maker and the code breaker for the first game. The code maker must then choose four numbers from a group of eight (usually one to eight) and arrange them in a particular order. They must keep this code a secret.

The code breaker then has their first chance to crack the code and writes down their guess. After each guess the code maker provides feedback next to each number indicating the following:

- A coloured-in dot indicates that a number is both correct and in its correct position in the code.
- A circle indicates that the number does appear in the code but is not in the correct position.
- A cross indicates the number does not appear in the code.

Once feedback has been given, the code breaker guesses again, and keeps going until the code has been broken. The code maker wins a point for each incorrect guess. The winner is the player with the most points after a pre-agreed number of games has been played.

✱ Variation

- To make the game harder, you can allow duplicate numbers to be used, so a player could even choose the same four code numbers.
- To make the game faster (and more complicated!), the players could be both code maker and code breaker at the same time, trying to guess their opponent's code at the same time as providing feedback on the guesses for their own.

" Things Grandpas Say "

If a job is worth doing, it is worth doing well.

Top Ten
Driving Songs

If boredom hits and the scenery is bleak, entertain each other with car-i-oke! Give your road trip soundtrack a topical mix by belting out a variety of car-themed tunes. Don't be afraid to sing your heart out and see if you can get other cars to join in! Here are 10 classic songs inspired by being on the road:

1. 'Drive My Car' – The Beatles

2. 'Cross Town Traffic' – Jimi Hendrix

3. 'Little Deuce Coupe' – Beach Boys

4. 'Greased Lightnin'' – John Travolta

5. 'Little Red Corvette' – Prince

6. 'Driving in My Car' – Madness

7. 'Drivin' South'– Jimi Hendrix Experience

8. 'Fast Car' – Tracy Chapman

9. 'Mustang Sally' – Wilson Pickett

10. 'Big Yellow Taxi' – Joni Mitchell

7 Which literary characters set out on a journey from the Tabard Inn, Southwark, in London?

8 Who is the Greek Goddess of Love?

9 The Meissen factory in Germany was one of the first manufacturers of which type of ceramic?

10 Who wrote the 'Twilight' series of novels?

Check the answers on pages 190-191.

Discarding 'throwing away' a card from your hand onto the discard pile. One card is discarded at the end of every turn.

Before play begins everyone must arrange their hands into potential sets and sequences. The player to the left of the dealer goes first and takes a card from the stock pile and adds it to their hand. When their turn is finished play passes to the left.

When it is your turn, if you have a meld you can lay it down, you can also lay off cards to melds already on the table, and then at the end you must throw away one card onto the discard pile. If you picked the top card from the discard pile at the beginning of your turn you are not allowed to discard that card during the same turn.

The first person to get rid of all their cards using the ways described above wins the hand.

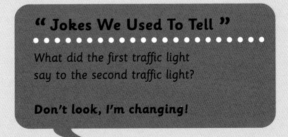

" Jokes We Used To Tell "
· ·
What did the first traffic light
say to the second traffic light?

Don't look, I'm changing!

Quiz Time
Answers

History
p. 30

1. The Bayeux Tapestry
2. Rome
3. The Treaty of Versailles
4. Hippocrates
5. Charles I
6. Christopher Columbus
7. Delano
8. Three: Catherine of Aragon, Kathryn Parr and Katherine Howard
9. Russia
10. Korea

Science and Nature
p. 66

1. Carbon
2. The femur (or thighbone)
3. Liquid Crystal Display
4. A Fibonacci Series
5. Protons and Neutrons
6. Lactose
7. The jaguar
8. X-rays
9. Cosine
10. Blue

" Jokes We Used To Tell "

What kind of car does Luke Skywalker drive?

A Toy-yoda!

Sport
p. 94

1. Ronaldo
2. Nadia Comaneci (Montreal in 1976)
3. San Francisco
4. Brian Lara (400 not out)
5. Lance Armstrong
6. Quidditch
7. Dressage, cross-country and show jumping
8. The high jump
9. 15
10. An Eagle

Geography
p. 160

1. The Balearic Islands
2. Peru
3. Washington DC
4. The Zambezi
5. The Dead Sea
6. An Oxbow lake
7. Singapore
8. Lebanon
9. The Indian Ocean
10. Gerard Mercator

Entertainment
p. 116

1. 'Mad Men'
2. 'Goodfellas'
3. Bon Jovi
4. Montague and Capulet
5. Lt Theo Kojak
6. Russell Crowe ('Gladiator')
7. Aaron
8. Casablanca
9. Gustav Holst
10. Kasabian

Art and Literature
p. 178

1. Jackson Pollock
2. 'Pride and Prejudice'
3. Auguste Rodin
4. King Lear
5. 'Little Women'
6. Frans Hals
7. The pilgrims in Chaucer's 'The Canterbury Tales'
8. Aphrodite
9. Porcelain
10. Stephenie Meyer

Acknowledgements

Katie Hewett

To me, games mean family, and I would like to thank mine for both testing out my carefully crafted instructions (I even found myself acting out the different signs for Charades to make sure I was describing them correctly), and for leaving me in peace while I attempted to get them down on paper. My five-year-old was delighted to be able to share the game Wink Murder with her friends at school. I am still waiting for my summons to the head teacher's office.

Thank you also to the friends and relations for all their encouragement and ideas. Finally, many thanks to Malcolm Croft, Rachel Malenoir and the team at Collins & Brown, for producing another lovely book.

Jo Pink

Many of the games in the book have been handed down from generation to generation, no doubt ever since Henry Ford first started turning out large volumes of the Model T and the car became the transport of the masses. Some are derivations of games that started life in the home long before the advent of television, and some, such as Bridge Baseball and Cow Football, have been committed to paper for the first time in this book. I believe that the game of Rock, Paper, Scissors even started life in another culture. The Japanese play Janken-pon with choki (scissors), paa (paper) and guu (rock) to decide who goes first instead of tossing a coin.

So a big thank-you to all the original creators of the games, many of which, like Chinese whispers, have taken on their own form over the years.

Most of all I'd like to thank my children; Theo, Isaac and Hetty for unwittingly testing out all the games over the last ten years.

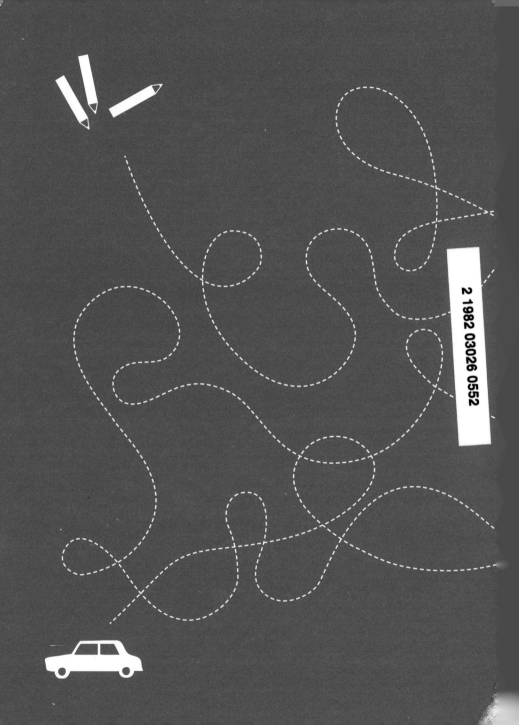

2 1982 03026 0552